my
PENTHOUSE
past

my
PENTHOUSE
past

FAILING MY WAY UP THE CORPORATE LADDER OF AN EMPIRE BUILT ON SKIN

a memoir by

Steve Belanger

not it publishing

My Penthouse Past:
Failing My Way Up The Corporate Ladder
Of An Empire Built On Skin
a memoir by Steve Belanger

Copyright © 2013 by Steve Belanger

Cover Photo: Timothy Devine
Cover Design: Wendy Russ
Interior Design: Natasha Fondren
Copyeditor: Gabriella West
Author Photo: Kristin Hoebermann

Published in the United States of America
First Printing, 2013

Print ISBN: 978-0-9891592-1-0
E-Book ISBN: 978-0-9891592-0-3

Not It Publishing
www.notitpublishing.com

Dedicated to my wife
for her unconditional love,
unwavering support and
questionable taste in men.

CONTENTS

Foreword   1

Preface   3

1: Introduction   5

2: A Brief History of *Penthouse Magazine*   9

3: A Brief History of Me   13

4: The Butterfly Effect   19

5: The Interview Process?   25

6: Time to Meet the Gang   31

7: Monday, Monday   35

8: Me and Bob G.   47

9: Week Two   55

10: Considering Other Options   59

11: Half-day Fridays!   63

12: Stevie's First Business Trip   67

13: How I Misspent Millions of Dollars   73

14: Personal Life?   79

15: The Gooch!   85

16: The Bosses of Me   87

17: The *Penthouse* Peeps   91

18: The Start of My Transformation   101

19: My First Pet of the Year Party   103

20: The Return of the RCE   107

21: Me, Interview Somebody?   111

22: Holy Overtime, Batman!   117

23: Moving Into NYC   121
24: Movin' On Up   123
25: My Life as a Financial Analyst   127
26: It's Game Time   131
27: How Had They Lasted This Long?   137
28: Showdown with the Queen   139
29: How Did This Happen?   143
30: Bar Jack   145
31: Howard Stern   149
32: Ring-Ring   153
33: *Penthouse Comix*   163
34: Finally Meeting Bob   171
35: Mo' Money, Mo' Problems   179
36: The Beginning of the End   181
37: And the Countdown Begins   185
38: Oooh, She's Pretty   191
39: Still Alive in '95   193
40: The End   197
Epilogue   201

ACKNOWLEDGMENTS

To Bob Guccione and all the folks who worked at *Penthouse Magazine* during my adventure. Without them this book would not exist.

To all of the wonderful creative people who helped me with the process of putting this book together: Stephen Parrish, Laurie Scheer, Debra Ginsburg, Wendy Russ, Natasha Fondren and Gabriella West.

To all of the individuals who have inspired me on my journey and boosted my confidence along the way: Richard Kline, Brett Cullen, William Hurt, Rick Rosenthal, Jay Mohr, Joel Stein, Henry Winkler, Jay Duplass, Mark Duplass, Alexander Ali, Bill Phillips, Andrew Daniels, Alice Martell, Peter Kelley and Tom Maley.

To MJP and FPL, gone too soon but always in my heart.

FOREWORD

S o, did you ever meet any of the *Penthouse* Pets?"
This would probably be the first question Larry Dallas, the swinging, hormonally imbalanced upstairs neighbor on *Three's Company,* might have asked Steve if they had met at the Regal Beagle. Well I guess literature imitates life, because I played that character in the iconic sit-com AND when I first met Steve, that was the second thing out of my mouth. The first was, "Should we split the check?"

In 2006, I had just moved from Los Angeles back to my home city, New York, and was teaching a sit-com workshop when our paths first crossed. Steve was one of my students and immediately I saw that he had talent and more importantly for a sit-com class, could actually bring humor to the material. He later applied the business acumen he so self-deprecatingly shares in this book to assist me in setting up my acting class, which is still going strong. He found the venue, kept the books and performed beautifully until he was somehow forced to leave due to impending father-hood. No hard feelings. Plus, he lived way the heck out on Long Island—a commute to try men's souls.

What is universally appealing about this book is two-fold. First, we have all had wacky, low-paying jobs before we found anything remotely permanent. They are detailed herein with a tremendous amount of hilarity and recognition. Secondly, it is one thing to want to leave the corporate lifestyle with its built-in perks, salary and, in this case, the glamour of an internationally branded publishing phenomenon to then go out and "do what I always wanted to do." Well, Steve took the leap. He is a writer. A writer with the wit and pop-culture acuity that always makes for interesting copy. He is also an actor, and a darn good one at that.

So enjoy this journey. Laugh. I did. And I never got a straight answer to the Pet question.

Ah, well…

Richard Kline

PREFACE

There I was in the lobby of *Penthouse Magazine* awaiting my first big job interview in New York City.

How did I get here?

It was the spring of 1988 and the city was still kind of a shithole. It wasn't the graffiti-covered dung heap it had been in the '70s when President Ford told it to drop dead, but it also wasn't the Disneyfied city it would become in a decade or so. Gaps and Baby Gaps were shooting up on every street corner, but window washers continued to pester any driver stuck at a red light and a stroll down Ninth Avenue would still allow you to see prostitutes and three-card monte hustlers plying their trade. The Manhattan of the late '80s was still a work in progress. So, as it turns out, was I.

1
INTRODUCTION

I began working for Bob Guccione's *Penthouse Magazine* when I was just 22 years old. I had already sampled a slew of different jobs by then, but this was the first big one. Somehow, without any real experience or knowledge of the industry, I managed to persevere and work my way up the ladder until I was released by the company eight years later.

Why have I chosen to tell this story now? To be honest, working at *Penthouse* had become just another chapter in the complex story of my life. In the nearly twenty years that have passed since I left, I've scaled even higher corporate heights, then tossed all that aside to pursue a career in writing and the performing arts. Add in marriage, children, tragedies and successes and there are any number of stories I could choose to tell. So why *Penthouse*? Why now?

It wasn't until Bob Guccione passed away back in 2010 that I started to really think about my time at *Penthouse*. When news of his passing spread, a lot of folks from my past reached out to me. Not *Penthouse* colleagues, but other folks who knew of my time there. It struck me that, to so many people, I was and forever would be "the guy that used to work at *Penthouse.*" *Why had that one fact stood out to so many people?* It made me think back to the time when working at *Penthouse* seemed like such a big deal to me. It was such an iconic brand and a huge part of this country's sexual culture for decades and my history would be forever tied to and defined by my tenure with Bob Guccione.

Regardless of what came after, *Penthouse* will always be where I spent the formative years of my young adulthood. By the time I turned thirty, I had spent more than a quarter of my life working for Mr. Guccione. I left there in 1995 and barely stayed in contact with anyone. The place quickly faded into my backstory, at least in my mind. Looking back now at how much my life changed during those years, it is apparent that I would not be where I am today without that experience. It was an odd, strange, confusing little journey, but one I remember fondly with zero regrets. I can proudly say that *Penthouse* made me the man I am today.

A QUICK NOTE ABOUT THIS MEMOIR

The memoir is easily the most maligned writing genre of the past decade. It seems like a lot of folks have gotten into trouble writing about some wondrous adventures they tried to pass off as true when, in fact, they weren't. James Frey, Lance Armstrong and so many others have, shall I say, stretched the truth to its breaking point. Was it to sell books? Gain notoriety? Cleanse their conscience? Had they convinced themselves that their yarns actually happened? It's a slippery little slope. I don't know how they are able to keep track of all of the various exaggerations and half-truths. Which is why they almost always get caught.

Fear not, dear reader. The story that unfolds here in these pixels is 100 percent accurate...as far as I know. Everything is expressed here exactly as I remembered it. Will everyone involved remember it exactly the same way? Probably not. Especially if they don't come off particularly well. But they also weren't witnessing these events through my eyes as a clueless young adult. What I lacked in knowledge and experience, I made up for with a keen eye, a pretty decent memory and the notion in the back of my head that someday these stories were going to come in really handy.

In order to not get any of my old colleagues in trouble, I have changed all of the names in this book except for the two folks in charge of the *Penthouse Magazine* empire, Bob Guccione and his wife, Kathy Keeton. They have now moved on to that big publishing house in the sky, so I don't think I will be hurting their chances at future employment by name-checking them here. I was not there for Guccione's meteoric rise to the top of the publishing world and his place in the Forbes 400, but I had a front row seat to the beginning of the end of the empire built on skin.

2
A BRIEF HISTORY OF
PENTHOUSE MAGAZINE
(BEFORE MY ARRIVAL)

Bob Guccione was an artist. At least, that was the label he always gave himself. Even at the peak of his considerable success, he still considered himself a painter who just happened to publish magazines. Born in Brooklyn, New York, in 1930 and raised in New Jersey, it was his love of the arts that set his life's course. He traveled the world in the late 1950s and '60s before settling down in London. He was never able to make a living from his canvases, but did find a burgeoning career in the magazine biz.

While working as the editor of a small weekly, he noticed a certain American magazine that seemed to be flying off British newsstands, Hugh Hefner's *Playboy*. This was Bob's magic moment. He realized that since *Playboy* had no local competition, if he could create a British equivalent to this bawdy men's magazine it would sell like gangbusters. He did not set out to build an empire; he was just hoping to provide the steady income that would finally allow him to continue his painting pursuits.

The first issue of *Penthouse Magazine* went on sale in early 1965. (Ironically, the same year I was born. Maybe our paths were destined to cross!) It sold out within a week. Bob had hoped the success would finance his painting endeavors, but he quickly found himself overwhelmed with the work of publishing a successful magazine. By the end of the decade it was doing extremely well, not just in Britain; it was also outselling *Playboy* two-to-one among American soldiers serving in Vietnam. This gave him the confidence to journey to America and take on *Playboy* head-to-head. Thus began the ascension of Bob Guccione.

The September edition in 1969 served as the premiere of *Penthouse* in America, but it was the April issue of 1970 that proved to be the true groundbreaker. It was the first issue to feature a picture of a woman's pubic hair. This may seem quaint, almost inconceivable, with today's constant sexual content overload; just turning on your computer or flipping through a few cable channels gives you access to endless nudity and sexual situations.

But back then it was a game-changer. For all the lewd, lascivious reputations imparted onto *Playboy* and the British *Penthouse* at the time, the nude models were still only revealing their bosoms and buttocks. The pubic area was always hidden away discreetly, yet seductively. That all changed with the glimpse of a young woman's pubis in that April 1970 issue. Subsequent pictorials were more and more audacious, and *Penthouse's* sales started to rise. Soon he was selling one million copies a month, then two million. By pushing the boundaries further and further with every issue, he had found a foolproof formula for success. Throughout the 1970s, the pictorials got racier and more graphic and the *Penthouse* coffers busted at the seams. In 1982, he was listed in the very first edition of the Forbes 400 list with a personal net worth of four hundred million dollars.

Flush with cash, this optimistic painter from Brooklyn quickly and zealously expanded his empire. He bought a building to house the company on New York's Upper West Side. He launched new magazines like *Omni* (a science fact-and-fiction hybrid) and expansions of the mothership like *Penthouse Forum*, *Penthouse Variations* and *Girls of Penthouse* (no distracting articles, just nudes, nudes and more nudes!). The stable also had mags about cars, photography, bodybuilding, one about national defense, even one that was intended to be a *Penthouse* for ladies called *Viva*. All the while, *Penthouse's* monthly circulation soared to over four million copies a month.

Bob's newfound extraordinary wealth allowed him to expand to other arenas as well. Among his extravagant investments was helping bankroll some impressive movies of the decade, including *Chinatown* and *The Longest Yard*. His first full foray into Hollywood filmmaking, the lavishly produced 1979 film *Caligula*, bombed at the box office (but the videotape release turned into a nice little profit center for the company in later years). He tried to open a *Penthouse* Casino in Atlantic City and he also invested millions in new energy technology. He was not a man with quiet dreams. He wanted to change the world, and for a while the success of the *Penthouse* brand afforded him that opportunity. It would not last forever.

3
A BRIEF HISTORY OF ME
(BEFORE ARRIVING AT *PENTHOUSE*)

As the son of divorced parents I spent my adolescence shuffling between both homes and learning to take care of myself. I got my first job at the age of fourteen and by the time I turned seventeen, I was itching to move on. Two weeks after my high school graduation I moved from Massachusetts to Connecticut. I may have wandered back home for a semester here, a summer there, but for the most part, I'd felt like I'd been living an adult life since I'd graduated high school.

This story starts when I was 22 years old. Like so many other post-collegiate kids, I thought I was much more worldly than I actually was. By 1988 I'd already been out of the house for a number of years, so I wasn't quite as out of my depth as some at that age. But I was still ill prepared for the fast-paced life in New York City.

I had a long list of careers I'd been piling up since I was fourteen, when I was hired as a landscaper for a local law firm. My boss had been the former mayor of our medium-sized city, which is impressive when I look back at it, but at the time, he was just the guy paying me three bucks an hour to do his yard work. I basically did all of the same chores the normal kid does at home, but I did it well enough that the guy soon promoted me to take care of the inside of the office as well. It was my first taste of success. It didn't come with a raise, but it meant that I would have a steady gig all winter long.

When I turned sixteen, I needed to ramp things up a bit, so I got a job as a gas station attendant. *Remember when kids would pump your gas, clean your windshield and check your oil? That was me!* It was my first experience working required shifts. At the lawyer's office, I would just go in and work until the job was done. Then I'd get paid and be gone. At the gas station I was on the clock, whether the place was bustling or hours went by without a customer. It wasn't bad in the summer, but the frigid Northeast winter meant I was standing out there dressed in endless layers of clothing to stay warm. The station also had an automatic car wash that I would have to run as well, which meant that every three minutes, I would get blasted by a quick spray of water from the machinery as I guided the cars through the array of brushes and hoses. One winter of this convinced me that I was not cut out for working outdoors. At least not in New England. If I'd been living in Florida or Arizona, maybe I'd still be working the pumps and soaking in the sun, but the cold weather chased me away.

After graduating from high school I decided to move out to Connecticut. I was going to start at Fairfield University there in the fall anyway, so I decided to get a head start and get a job. My first gig was as a barback at a popular seafood restaurant. My primary responsibility was to keep the beer supply cold and the ashtrays clean. I excelled at both. So much so, that I was promoted to busboy. I'll be honest with you, nobody cleared a table better. Bussing tables meant much better tips and, like my promotion at the lawyer's office, started me on a trend of upward career mobility that stuck with me for years.

After needing a break from work to focus on my freshman studies, I then found myself a summer job as a short order cook. I had applied for a busboy gig, but the owner saw something in me that made him think I could work in the kitchen. He gave me a menu to study and had me working the grill the next day. It was a smallish restaurant called The Pie Plate and they were known more for their baked goods that, luckily, I had no hand in. They offered a basic menu, heavy on club sandwiches, burgers and the like, but it was still pretty challenging to me. Even more overwhelming was that after just a one-day training session, the guy left me to work the grill all by myself. It was truly trial by fire, grease fire. I sweated through the first few days, probably angering more than my share of waiting diners, but I eventually got the hang of it. It helped me become a pretty decent little cook and I still make a helluva patty melt.

When the next school year started, I couldn't keep up with the restaurant hours so I took an on-campus job at our big recreation center. I was the gym's laundry guy. Now, regardless of what you've heard, washing sweat-soaked towels all day is not as fulfilling as it sounds. It was another mindless, clock-watching job that reminded me a lot of the gas station, except I was warm and smelled of fabric softener.

I then thought I'd found a good job working at a supermarket as a shelf-stocker. It was eight hours a night on the graveyard shift stacking cans, but it let me keep up with my studies. I quickly found that working nights and sleeping days proved quite a burden on my schoolwork. The vampire hours were messing with my body clock, especially when we'd have a few after-work beers at eight o'clock in the morning.

One summer during college I actually went back home to Massachusetts and spent three months working in a factory. It was a metal-processing plant and I spent every day as a mindless lemming. I punched the clock at 7:30 AM, and loaded anodized aluminum onto racks for two hours until the whistle blew for our ten-minute coffee break. Then back to the line until the whistle blew for our thirty-minute lunch. Then the afternoon dragged on until the 3:50 PM whistle that meant we had five minutes to wash the chemicals off our bodies and punch out for the end of the day. Life in the factory was not nearly as glamorous as that Billy Joel song makes it sound, but it was a great experience and taught me that I definitely wanted more out of life.

My next job was about as far from the grunt physical labor of the factory as I could get. I became a waiter at the Fairfield Country Club: a hoity-toity joint full of Connecticut's wealthiest folks. It was my first experience kissing the asses of rich white guys. (Sadly, not my last.) It taught me that personality and charm could get you a long way. I found it easy to swallow my pride and suck up to these folks, which made me really good at my job.

In the middle of my senior year of college, I ran out of money. Unable to afford tuition, I put my education on hold and ventured out into the real world. I took the first thing offered me and got my first full-time office job as a computer programming associate. It was a pretty fancy title when you consider that my main function was to sit next to the giant office printer and make sure it didn't jam. Which it did, just about every four minutes. It wasn't glamorous, but it was a real job in a real office and felt like what grown-ups were supposed to be doing for a living. I was 21;

I still didn't know what I wanted to be when I grew up, but I had made a few stops along the way that taught me what I definitely did *not* want to do.

My big problem with the office job is that it wasn't really paying the bills. I didn't need a ton of money, but I needed more than I was making. At this point I was living in a small house in Stamford, Connecticut, with four other guys I'd gone to college with. They all had jobs in the disciplines they'd gone to school for and were on the right career paths. I had been majoring in psychology when I left school, not because I wanted to go into that field, but because I found those classes to be the most interesting. Now that choice was starting to look like a big mistake.

In need of some extra cash, I took a part-time gig working as a Macy's sales associate at the Stamford store. They put me in the Menswear Department, but I didn't last very long. My sweater-folding skills were found lacking by management.

It was at this point that my old boss from the country club called me in for a meeting. Their restaurant manager had quit and he wanted me to take over. The job paid a good deal more than I was making at my office gig and if I were only thinking short-term, I would have jumped at it in a second. But I didn't. In the seven years I'd been working since that first job at the age of fourteen, I had never turned down a job that was offered to me. For some reason, this offer gave me pause. It was a better job for the moment, but for the first time I was thinking of the future. If I stuck with the office job, for a few years I didn't know what opportunities would arise, but if I took the gig managing the restaurant, it would probably lead, if anything, to more restaurant work in the future and a lifetime in the service industry. It seemed crazy at the time, but I turned them down. I stuck with my menial office job and hoped for the best.

My efforts were rewarded just a few months later when I was promoted to computer programmer. More upward mobility! I didn't know a thing about computers, but I was willing to learn. They taught me how to write computer code...for actual programs! I didn't know what the hell I was doing. I may have invented the Internet, I'm not sure. You're welcome.

Those are the many and varied career steps (and missteps) that led me to sitting in the lobby of Bob Guccione's empire in my ill-fitting Sunday suit.

I was reaching my one-year anniversary in that computer programmer job in the spring of 1988. I didn't hate it, but I didn't love it either. I still had no clue what I wanted to be when I grew up, but I was pretty sure it didn't involve sitting in a windowless room in Westport, Connecticut, working on computer-tabulation programs. It's important to note that, technically, I didn't actually "write" the programs. I just reformatted the programs we had for whatever client they gave me. I still have no idea how to write anything more than a grammatically incorrect memoir.

One balmy night that spring I was out drinking with an old buddy of mine from college. It was, without any hyperbole, THE NIGHT THAT WOULD CHANGE MY LIFE FOREVER. (Dear reader, if you can, please read that last sentence in your loudest, spookiest voice while possibly playing some scary thunderstorm effects in the background. Thank you.)

4
THE BUTTERFLY EFFECT

The Butterfly Effect is a phenomenon in chaos theory that states, "When a butterfly flaps his wings in Myanmar, a taxicab runs over a pigeon in NYC." Or something like that. I may not have my facts quite up to snuff when it comes to scientific theory, but I do know that many things led up to that one night in a bar that would lead me to a new career in porn.

Here's the progression: A copywriter at *Penthouse,* a gentleman I never met, got fired. My college buddy, Jack, who was already working in the production department at *Penthouse,* desperately wanted to work in advertising. Jack got hired as the new copywriter, but his old bosses wouldn't let him take the new job full time until they hired his replacement. This made Jack cranky enough to want to go out and get drunk. He called his old college buddy (me!) to get drunk with him.

We sat there, drinking our cheap, domestic draft beers, watching baseball and trading *woe is me* work stories. At some point, not unlike Bob Guccione himself decades earlier, Jack had a magic moment of his own. He looked like the cat that ate the canary.

The wonderful, beer-infused idea that struck him was quite simple. He said, "Why don't you take my old job?"

It seemed like a great idea at the time, but then again, a lot of things sound great when you've been in a bar for four hours on a Tuesday night watching West Coast baseball until one in the morning. He explained what the job entailed. He had been a Production Analyst (*sounded vague enough!*) and had something to do with the physical manufacturing of the magazines. Not much of what he said made sense, except the part where he explained that up to that point, all of their reports and inventory were still mostly written by hand and then done up on typewriters. Management was hoping to computerize their whole record-keeping process. Remember, this was 1988: IBM's Selectric typewriters were still the norm in most offices. I had no clue what being a Production Analyst entailed, but at the time, I didn't really know what I was doing anyway in my current gig as a programmer. Since both jobs involved computers, I figured maybe I should give it a shot. Plus...it was *Penthouse*!

I'll be the first to confess that working for *Penthouse* itself was quite a charismatic draw. I wasn't all hopped up because it was a girlie mag and I was some super–horny perv who wanted to stare at naked women all day, but I wasn't that far removed from the 11-year-old boy whose head almost exploded the first time he'd seen a *Penthouse Magazine*.

Women might not understand the huge rite of passage that it is, but seeing boobies (and more!) for the first time, even in print form, is still mind-blowing to any young male. I remember playing doctor with the girl next door when I was no more than five or six, and the female form was nothing more than an anomaly to me. It was an odd, funny, different-looking kind of a thing.

But as adolescence crept up, I remember looking at girls a little bit differently. Then one morning, I saw my future. Before school everyday, I used to go to my friend Kevin's house. He was a latch-key kid like myself and his mom would leave for work early, so I'd go over there at seven in the morning and we'd have a half hour or so to hang around and do what 11-year-olds do. Mostly we sat around reading comics or listening to his KISS albums. He's the one who indoctrinated me into the KISS army.

But one morning was special. He had swiped a copy of *Penthouse* from his older brother. That day's thirty minutes flew by as we stared at the magazine's glossy photos of beautiful, naked women. We giggled, like schoolboys do, and pretended to know more about what we were looking at than we really did. I bounded up his stairs the next morning, eager to stare at the pictures again, but we were busted. Kevin's brother caught him going through his stuff and locked them away forever. It would be a while before I would see pictures like that again, and even longer until I saw anything like that in the flesh, but I was hooked.

Even so, the nude ladies weren't the reason I was so enticed by *Penthouse*. It was the name, the brand and the cachet. Star-struck isn't the right word, but it's close. As a small kid I was a TV addict, a magazine nerd and a movie fiend. I was a pop-culture junkie before there really was such a thing. My first real exposure to this feeling was years earlier when a college friend of my sister had gotten an entry-level gig at *People Magazine*. That was surreal to me. Here was this person, someone I'd actually met, who was working at *People Magazine*! I would show her name on the masthead to my friends. Why? I have no idea. I didn't even know I wanted to be a writer back then, let alone that I'd spend close to two decades working in magazine publishing. It was just the fact that she was a real part of that special world. In the small city in Massachusetts where I was born, most folks' big dreams consisted of growing up and maybe working in Boston. I wanted more than that. I just had no idea how to get there. After I went to college in Connecticut and moved to the Stamford area just outside of NYC, I still didn't know what I wanted to be, but I was certainly getting closer to the real world. The big city.

When I was a kid, magazines were like the movies or TV to me—they were made somewhere special like New York or Hollywood. Places so far removed from my day-to-day existence that they almost didn't seem real. So later, when my college buddy Jack started working at *Penthouse*, it was mind-blowing to me. Just a few years earlier I was a gas jockey working the pumps at a Texaco station for a few bucks an hour. My whole life was ahead of me, but I didn't have a clue where I was going.

I still consider myself very lucky at this point that I'd been such a loser with the ladies back then. My lack of confidence and too-tall, too skinny physique left me quite unsuccessful when it came to getting any affection, or attention for that matter, from anyone of the female persuasion. I say I was fortunate because if for some reason some sexy schoolgirl had gotten herself a case of the "Stevies" and allowed me to, as they say in the Bible, lay down with her, that would have been it for me. I'm sure I would have been married by twenty and never left my hometown, which I'd seen so many of my peers do. *Would I have regretted it?* Who knows? I think I would have, but maybe I would have never realized I was missing out on anything. Fortunately, the female sex voted unanimously to keep me away from sealing the deal, and I went off to college. (*I didn't have much more success with the ladies there either, but enough to keep me moving up the depth chart.*)

So when Jack said, "Why don't you take my old job?" I jumped at the chance. I didn't know what was waiting for me out in the world, but I had the sense that it was something special and that I just needed to make a big leap. It could have been an internship at a TV network or an entry-level job at some book company. It just seemed that a gig in the world of media was the right thing for me and I was determined to roll the dice with the first opportunity that presented itself.

5
THE INTERVIEW PROCESS?

Jack's brilliant idea happened late on a Tuesday night and by 9:30 the next morning, still working through the haze of a mid-week hangover, he called to tell me to come into the city to interview for the job that afternoon. I went to my boss, lied and said I had an afternoon doctor's appointment (*probably easy to believe since I was pasty and sweaty from the prior night's festivities, but back then I was almost always pasty and sweaty from the prior night's activities*). I scooted home, put on my ill-fitting Sunday suit and jumped on a train to Manhattan.

I'm not exactly a fashion plate now, but I can wear the hell out of a nice Brooks Brothers suit. Back then, my wardrobe consisted of khaki pants that were never quite long enough for my long, lanky frame and a button-down dress shirt. It was exactly the clothing that was required by my high school's dress code and it remains my signature look to this day. So the only suit I had was one my mother had bought for me a year or two earlier, sight unseen. She must have described me to the suit guy at the store and he sold her a pair of mix-and-match coordinates since my measurements were a bit odd. Being six-foot-three and weighing 160 pounds ensured that I would never be able to buy a suit off the rack without tons of alterations. So what she bought me what was basically a Garanimals suit with a jacket made for a skinny boy and pants made for a giant stick figure. It fit me exactly like you would think a suit bought 200 miles away for an oddly shaped man *would* fit. The jacket hung boxily on my narrow shoulders and the pants were baggy and had way too much fabric in the waist and crotch area. I looked like David Byrne's dumber younger brother.

On the way into Manhattan on the train, I reviewed my pathetic excuse for a resume. At the time, I was pretty proud of what I'd put together. I wish I still had a copy of it. *How the hell could I have even filled an entire page? How many sentences did it take me to describe my towel-washing position?*

As I nervously made my way from Grand Central Terminal to the Upper West Side of Manhattan, what I didn't know was that the best thing I had going for me was what was going on over at *Penthouse.* My buddy Jack was so determined to fill his old position that he spent the whole day building up me and my abilities with the powers that be. It also helped that his superiors were kind of clueless.

The interview process began with a quick meet and greet with the guy who would soon become my boss, Howard Hobner. He was a short, stocky guy, but judging from the pictures all over his office, he sure loved his golf. *How could a busy Manhattan executive find enough time to play so much golf.* I would find out soon enough.

"Jack says you're a real whiz at computers. Is that true?" Howard asked.

A whiz I definitely was not.

"Yes sir. I write computer code for tabulation programs for a market research company."

I had been rehearsing that line all morning and even I was impressed with how smart it made me sound. I feared any follow-up question he might fire at me about computers, but that was it. The rest of our chat consisted of small talk. Howard seemed pleased with me. He was impressed that I worked on computers. That was it. He didn't ask any further details. Jack had vouched for me and I knew computers—that was enough to pass the first test.

Then Howard brought his boss in for a quick chat. He was a cheeky, smooth-talking Brit who rambled on for ten minutes about the importance of the position. He also wanted to point out what a big mistake he thought Jack was making by leaving his tutelage and going off to work in advertising. Since I nodded my head appropriately and didn't interrupt, I unbelievably had passed the second test.

Next, it was time for my third and final test. They brought me in to meet with their resident computer expert (RCE). And, no joke, he was exactly what you would think of if someone said the phrase "resident computer expert." He was an overweight bear of a man with a gray, scraggly beard and a dandruff-y head of hair. He wore a stained short-sleeved shirt. The fabric had that look of worn motel sheets that have been washed thousands of times. He looked uncannily like the Comic Book Guy from *The Simpsons*, at least what I could see of him in the eerie green glow emitted by his computer that was the only light source in his dark, unventilated, windowless bunker of an office. My fifteen minutes with him were the most confusing of my life.

Yes, I worked on computers every day, but I mostly did exactly what I'd been told to do, without really knowing how or why. I was simply one of Pavlov's dogs, salivating on cue at my keyboard. The one big thing Jack had prepped me on was to tell them I was fluent at Lotus 1-2-3. I didn't even know what that meant, but when I said it during my earlier chats it had been accepted blindly. "Oh, okay, good, that's perfect," everyone responded.

Lotus 1-2-3 was a spreadsheet application, an early version of Microsoft Excel. It was, it turned out, the most important requirement for the position. They wanted to convert their inventories, analysis and work schedules over to a Lotus system. The only problem was that I didn't know what the hell it was and their computer guy could tell right away. He probably smelled my fear before we started, even through the haze of cigarette smoke that wafted about his desk. He asked me a few Lotus questions, which I couldn't even come close to faking my way around. Frustrated, he finally just asked me to explain what I did at my current computer job. I couldn't even do that! I explained what the company did. We were a computer tabulation company that compiled the results of national marketing polls. *Sounds sexy, doesn't it? No wonder I wanted to leave!*

He kept asking pointed questions about what kind of machine I worked on and the best answer I could come up with was "beige." Frustrated, he gruffly dismissed me back to reception while he went to go chat with Howard. I sat there figuring I should just leave. The elevators were right there; I could just hop on the next one that opened. I was never going to get the job after that pitiful performance. All that would happen is that the boss would come back and yell at me for pretending to know stuff I didn't. It would be like every time I got in trouble at school. I hated getting in trouble. I couldn't wait for the damn elevator to open! Then Howard came back to the lobby and brought me back to his office.

I was ready to get reamed. *Could he have this put on my personal record? Did I even have a personal record?*

He told me to have a seat, then he shut the door to his office. *Uh-oh.* Nothing good ever happens behind closed doors. As I braced myself for the worst, he started talking. And talking and talking. At least he wasn't yelling. Finally, I started actually listening to the guy. He was offering me the job! *How was that possible?* I was being offered a computer position even though their resident expert had obviously just told him I didn't know shit about computers. That was like hiring the guy who can't tread water in the pool to be a beach lifeguard. But there it was...the guy was offering me the job and an annual salary of $24,000 a year. *Holy crap!* I accepted it on the spot. We shook hands, looked at a calendar to figure out which day I would start (after giving two weeks' notice at my old place) and that was it. Just like that I was back on the elevator, whistling a happy tune.

Now I know I did the absolute worst thing by accepting the job immediately. Everyone says you're supposed to take a day or two to think about it, but I didn't. I did the first thing that came to my head, I accepted. It was crazy, considering the fact that just twenty-four hours earlier I was heading to Happy Hour complaining about my old job, and here I was strolling down Broadway with a brand-spanking-new profession. Of course, my new bosses weren't too smart either. They hired me without checking any references, calling any old bosses or you know, proving that I could actually do the job. I would later learn that Howard understood computers even less than I did, so whatever his computer expert told him about me went right over his head.

In a Groucho Marx–like conundrum, I should never have taken a job at a company that would hire me for that position.

But they offered it, I accepted it and the die was cast. All of us clueless idiots forging ahead together under our fearless leader, Bob Guccione. What could possibly go wrong?

The next morning I gave notice at my old job and that was that. I spent the two intervening weeks buying some new work clothes, a monthly train pass and making preparations for my daily commute. Since a few of the guys I was living with in the house also commuted into the city everyday, it was going to be a tough schedule getting all of us out the door for early trains.

In a slight harbinger of the financial doom that I was about to dive into, I realized that I'd actually made quite a sizable error myself. The 24,000 they offered seemed like a huge jump from the eighteen thou I was making in Connecticut, but after deducting the cost of commuting, the additional taxes and everything else, I ended up with less take-home money in my pocket at the end of every week. Add in the much higher cost of eating and hanging out in the city and I was soon going to be poorer than I'd ever been in my life. Which is saying something.

6
Time to Meet the Gang

The Friday before I was supposed to start my new job, Jack invited me into the city to join the *Penthouse* gang for Happy Hour. Surprisingly, I wasn't all that nervous about meeting my new co-workers. Since I'd kind of slipped past the higher-up gatekeepers earlier in the process, I thought I'd have no problem being accepted by this group of soon-to-be peers. Once again, I was wrong.

The bar we met at was a block away from the office and would become a regular hangout for the next several years. (It's not there anymore. To paraphrase Joni Mitchell, they put up a Reebok Sports Club where my watering hole used to be.) The motley crew was made up of secretaries, entry-level folks and assorted middle managers. The first thing I noticed right away were the women. I was still mostly running with my college crowd back in Connecticut, so my encounters with the fairer sex all tended to be pretty similar. Fresh-faced, nice girls just starting to experience the adult life. The women I'd soon be working with weren't that. They were confident and brassy and fit right into the fast-paced

New York City lifestyle. They all seemed more, for lack of a better word, worldly.

In my mind I thought I was worldly too, but I most certainly was not. This group had lived and worked together in Manhattan for the better part of their twenties. As for me, if you added up a few concerts at Madison Square Garden, a trip to Radio City with my parents as a four-year-old (to see the original *True Grit*!), and my interview two weeks prior, this was probably only my sixth trip in to the Big Apple, ever. But for some reason, I felt I belonged.

This new crew accepted me easily enough. They were friends with Jack. I was Jack's friend. Ergo, "Welcome! Drink up!" But after the initial "Where you from? Where did you work before?" banter, they quickly grew tired of me. I can't blame them. At that point in my life I didn't bring a whole lot to the table conversationally (some would argue that I still don't). I sat back and tried to soak in the experience. And as many beers as possible. What struck me the most was that almost to a fault, every guy was chock-full of confidence. As I'd soon learn, it's hard not to work all day in the shadow of male swagger that is *Penthouse* and not carry it around with you as a proud badge of honor. The women were a confident lot, too. They had to be, to work at *Penthouse*. They had to deal with their share of chauvinism around the office, but I'm sure it was much worse out in the real world every time they told some guy where they worked.

That night, on the late train home, I was suddenly overwhelmed by the sense that I was extremely ill prepared for this new adventure I'd begun. I felt like a kid who'd just been bumped up from Double-A ball straight to the Majors. Sure, the game was still basically the same, it just moved infinitely faster. How would

I fit in with these new people, who were all basically *real* adults? Not mature, per se…but they seemed to have their shit together a lot more than the awkward twenty-two-year-old who still lived in a tiny house with a bunch of his college buddies. Had I made a huge mistake? Monday was just two days away.

7
Monday, Monday

Up until this moment, in all of the myriad jobs and enterprises I had been involved in, I had never lived more than ten minutes from where I worked. This made getting up, out the door and to my post a pretty straightforward process. Those days were gone. I now had a ninety-minute door-to-door commute to deal with. Like everything else, I got used to it eventually and passed the time reading the paper, doing crosswords or dozing off. But for those first few weeks, each trip into and out of the city felt like I was taking the red-eye to Los Angeles. It was cramped, exhausting and endless. Especially on that first morning. I was squashed in between two train-commuting veterans who weren't going to give up an inch of space to a tall, gangly neophyte, no matter how uncomfortable I looked.

The ride went even slower with the added stress of not really knowing what I'd gotten myself into. The spreadsheet thing still had me scared. In the two weeks since I'd gotten the job, I actually had a friend teach me some Lotus 1-2-3 basics, so I was hopeful I could at least start figuring things out once I got there. As long as I stayed away from the RCE, I thought I could work it out. I sat on the train and went over my notes for what felt like hours. I was finally distracted by the conductor announcing the Larchmont stop. Larchmont? I was barely halfway there! Son of a ...

My new commute consisted of a one-hour ride on Metro North Railroad, then a quick ride on the Times Square Shuttle over to 7th Avenue, and then a three-stop jaunt uptown on the ONE train to 66th Street. An annoying little adventure that in time I could do half-asleep, but on Day One I did with the steely cool of a high school freshman who can't quite read his class schedule. I thought I was golden until, while sitting on the ONE train, I realized that the first few stops looked unfamiliar. And the numbers were getting lower, not higher. *I got on the wrong effing train!* We were at 18th Street before I could jump off to try and correct my mistake. I now had ten minutes to get to my first day on the job and I was almost fifty blocks from my destination. I ran across the street and had to use another subway token to go back uptown. That was half my lunch money! I sweated through the long subway ride and found myself racing through the lobby at 9:15.

I assumed that when I got off the elevator, my new boss would be standing there pointing to his watch with a disappointed shake of his head. The doors opened and... he was not there. No one was there. No one except for the scary security guard. He sat there at an ornate, if slightly gaudy desk, which looked too good to hold the *New York Post* that he was currently devouring with a scholar's eye. He looked up and gave me the once-over like a street cop eyeing a perp. In fact, he was a cop. A retired one. *Penthouse* had a small security staff composed entirely of retired cops. One was posted on each floor and a few more protected Bob Guccione's house. They all wore the same uniform of tan slacks and brown polyester sport coats. They also all wore the same slack-jawed look of bored frustration. As he stared me down, I could already feel my voice going up a few octaves, until I finally broke the silence with a very high-pitched, "Hi, today's my first day. I'm going to be working for Howard Hobner." He looked me over wearily, then picked up the phone and punched in a few numbers. "Yeah, I got a kid here for Howie."

He went back to his paper and I just kind of meandered. I strolled over to the same couch I'd waited on nervously two weeks earlier for my interview. Now I was actually here as a real *Penthouse* employee. Everything had seemed so nice that first time. White leather couches, gold-trimmed walls and lighting fixtures, granite floors. As I waited nervously the second time, I got a closer look at things and realized things weren't as glamorous as I'd thought. The leather couches were actually closer to lightly stained vinyl pleather. The gold trim everywhere was quite tarnished in a lot of spots. The place was spotless, but it was easy to see that everything had aged. Kind of like the *Penthouse* brand itself.

I looked over at the security guard again, and for the first time saw the gun he had holstered to his hip. *They have armed guards here? What the hell for?*

While I sat there trying to contemplate the need for an armed militia on every floor, a woman finally came out to get me. "Steve? I'm Annette. Come on in." The security guard barely looked up as she he led me into the inner offices. She explained that she was the secretary for the Cheeky Brit. My mind started racing. *Was she bringing me back to see him? Where was Howard? Did the RCE finally get through to him and tell him I wasn't fit for the position?*

Are they pissed that I'm so late on my first day? Am I going to be back out on the street in five minutes without a job? Why does that guy have a gun?!

Before any more panic could swell up inside me, we'd arrived at our destination. A dingy beige cubicle in a sea of other dingy beige cubicles. Annette led me in. "Here you go. Howard's not in today, but he said you should just go ahead and get started." Then she turned and left. Huh?!

I really thought it was a joke. Like I was on some bizarre episode of *Candid Camera* (*Punk'd* was still fifteen years from existence, kids). I sat in the chair and tried to take in my surroundings. The cabinets above the cubicle were lined with every magazine we published in chronological order. The row of *Penthouse Magazines* was a porn collector's dream. Then there was a stack of their digest-sized books, *Penthouse Forum* & *Penthouse Variations*, as well as their newest magazine, *Penthouse Hot Talk*. In another cabinet, which I'm guessing was the scholarly side, was every issue of *Omni Magazine*. I wasn't very familiar with that one but I remember the cool kids in my high school reading it. That made me think back a bit to what my younger self would think if someone had told him, when he was a boobie-obsessed thirteen-year-old, that in the not-too-distant future, he'd be sitting in the middle of enormous stacks of endless erotica. Every issue of *Penthouse* lay before me, including I'm sure the very first one I'd ever seen that day a little over a decade earlier which my friend Kevin had stolen from his brother.

I spun around in my chair like a Bond villain and tried to figure out what to do. I turned on the hulking grey computer and when it stirred to life with an unbelievably loud "BEEEEP!" I assumed someone would come yell at me. No one did. I had that fear for most of my first few months, that someone would come yell at me, realize I was a sham and throw me out on the street. Not a great way to start a career.

The computer screen slowly grew brighter, but all it gave me was four simple characters,

$$C:\backslash>$$

followed by a blinking cursor.

I knew they worked off an early version of Windows, but I didn't know how to get there from this ominously simple screen. I felt like the constantly blinking cursor was mocking me, inviting me to enter a command that would no doubt fail. After a lengthy staring contest with said cursor, I decided to at least try typing W-I-N-D-O-W-S to see if that would work, but I only got as far as W-I-N-D before deleting it, all for fear that it would set off an error alarm louder than the initial beep. I decided to lay low and read the company directory that was on the desk by the phone. Yes, on the first day of my new job, I was literally reading the phone book.

After what seemed like hours of boredom, I looked at the clock. 9:30. *Uh-oh.* Had I somehow stepped into a black hole where time is absorbed at an infinitely slower rate? The day had barely begun and I was already exhausted and had no clue what to do with myself. Then it finally hit me! My buddy Jack, who had done this job for a year, was right upstairs; I'll just ask him what to do! I figured out how to dial another extension on the phone system (really, nothing was simple back then). Jack was thrilled with his shiny new job as an advertising copywriter and really didn't want to deal with his old gig anymore, but said he'd try and swing down later and show me the ropes. Okay, that was a step in the right direction. One more glance at the clock... 9:31.

What to do? I was done trying to figure out the computer. I was afraid if I started mucking round and screwed up, sirens might go off and a huge net would fall on me from the ceiling. I opened a few of the drawers and found some files that seemed interesting, but none of them made much sense to me, so I left them alone, too. I looked around again at the stacks of reading material that surrounded me. I had the urge to grab a *Penthouse* and take a peek, but that didn't seem like the right thing to do at work. Even though I now worked AT *Penthouse*. In the interest of research, I grabbed an *Omni* and started reading it. It was a science fact-and-fiction magazine and I wasn't a very big fan. Sure, I geeked out to *Star Wars* like every other kid growing up in the '70s, but I couldn't get into the magazine's content. The science articles were about nuclear fusion and quantum physics and other stuff that went right over my head. Even the science fiction was too highbrow for me, so I slipped the *Omni* back into the rack while fighting a terrible case of the yawns.

My body was still adjusting to the early morning wake-up and long commute. No breakfast and no coffee had me ready to pass out by the time 10 AM rolled around. Since I'd been mostly ignored here on my new island of isolation, I decided I had no other choice but to give my brain a quick hit of stimulation by perusing a *Penthouse*. I grabbed one at random and flipped slowly through the pages. I didn't stay on any one page too long for fear of getting caught staring at a picture of a naked lady. I eventually paused on one of the articles and decided to give it a read. It was something about Israel and the Palestinian state. *Jeez, is this what the articles are really about?* I continued to flip and finally landed on the first pictorial. That's when it finally, truly, sank in. I work for *Penthouse Magazine*. *Yikes.*

It seemed cool in theory when I took the job, but now looking at the pictures in the bright light of day (or actually the dim light of a humming fluorescent), for the first time it felt a little weird. As I contemplated these new thoughts while staring at a picture of buxom young woman doing a headstand, I suddenly heard a voice from behind me. "What are you looking at you perv?!!" she shouted. I turned to see a very attractive girl, maybe a few years older than myself, standing there. I started to stammer and stutter and she just laughed. "Hi, I'm Susie." Embarrassed, I just stared back. "I'm a friend of Jack's, we met at Happy Hour the other night."

"Oh right. Susie. Of course! Hi, how's it going?" I still had no clue who she was; I met so many people that night. But I didn't care, she was cute and friendly, and most importantly she was talking to me! A respite from my solitary confinement in cubicle hell.

We made some small talk, and then I embarrassed myself again by not being able to stifle a big yawn. I apologized and asked her where I could get myself a cup of coffee. "Didn't Jack or someone give you the tour yet?"

"Not really," I said shyly.

"Typical for this place. Come on, I'll show you around." And she did, she showed me the coffee room (*important!*), the bathrooms (*even more important!!*) and kind of gave me the lay of the land, pointing out a few people I sort of recognized from the bar the other night. We continued making small talk along the way and if this had been a typical '80s movie, the character of me (played by a young John Cusack) would have won her over with sparkling dialogue, a brief glimpse of my inner dark side and a hysterical wit that would hold the promise of years of entertainment. But it wasn't an '80s movie and by the time we headed back to my cubicle, I could already tell she had grown bored of me. She was a city-smart girl wise to the ways of the world and I was the clueless rube from Connecticut who just spent five minutes talking about Huey Lewis music. *Idiot!*

As I went back to my desk, she waved a non-committal goodbye and her conversation just drifted off like an audible ellipse. My "Thanks for the tour!" trailed after her shadow and fell on deaf ears. And just like that I was alone again. The magical '80s movie connection was not to be. After her quick judgment call in that first ten minutes, she decided I had nothing to offer. She was probably right. Our only communication for the next eight years would be a smiling nod as we passed each other in the halls. *Who says first impressions aren't important?*

Eschewing the weirdness I'd felt about looking at the *Penthouse* mags earlier in the morning, I now rifled through two years worth of issues. It only took about forty minutes for the allure of the naked pictures to wear off. It was shocking how quickly the fascination dissipated. Maybe it was because there was such a vast array to choose from that the taboo was now gone, and with it the desire. Don't get me wrong, I still loved the *idea* of naked women, but staring at pictures of them for hours at a time? Turns out it wasn't my thing. Before long I would be comparing working there to working at a donut shop...the first morning is great as you gorge yourself on all the free donuts, but pretty soon you never want to see another chocolate-glazed again. And that's how it was with the girlie pics.

I eventually started flipping past the pictorials looking for something to read. Luckily, I found that mixed in with the pictorials they actually did have some pretty decent articles (Middle Eastern politics aside.) A profile of David Gilmour talking about his Pink Floyd days and a mob informant who worked for the FBI kept me entertained for the better part of the morning.

Finally, at around 11:30, Jack came down. Not a moment too soon either. I was seconds away from falling asleep at my desk. He didn't have a ton of time because he had to get back upstairs. I should have realized then that my new job must really suck if he was so desperate to get away from it. He was now a copywriter up in the advertising promotions department. I wasn't sure what that meant, but he said he wanted to be more creative.

But for now, he showed me just enough about my job as a Production Analyst so that I could keep up appearances. My main duties were budget reports and paper inventory. For the budget stuff I just had to write up an analysis of how much each issue of every magazine had cost to produce once all the bills had come in. He showed me the drawer full of previous reports (which I had cluelessly looked through earlier) and gave me the broad strokes of how they were done. The paper inventory part seemed a little tougher. I was supposed to order and keep track of all of the paper used to print all of our magazines. *Penthouse* alone produced millions of copies each month. Add in all of the other titles and we were looking at literally tons and tons of paper. Jack showed me the order forms, but I had trouble comprehending that I would be placing orders for millions of dollars worth of paper. Surely someone with more knowledge and experience should be in charge of that! Would you let a kid with forty-four dollars in his bank account be in charge of millions of dollars worth of purchases?

Like he did with the budget sheets, Jack just showed me some examples and told me to keep doing it like he'd done it. Then he left, back to solve some advertising copywriter emergency upstairs. I stared at the pile of folders and papers in front of me. I was still pretty clueless but at least I had a starting point.

After reading Jack's past budget reports, I started seeing how repetitive most of it was and figured I could keep doing the same type of thing. As I said, in my last job as a computer programmer, I basically just took the company's programs and reformatted them for whatever client I was working on. It seemed like I could get away with the same thing here. I just had to study what Jack had done in prior months and repeat the process. I could totally do that!

Emboldened, I figured it was time to take my lunch break. I strolled around the neighborhood. The office was at 66th and Broadway, so Lincoln Center was just around the corner. Part of me was still amazed that I was working in New York City. I was strolling around the Lincoln Center fountain just like those kids from *Fame* (not the movie, but the TV version). This was where they had shot *West Side Story*. I could look downtown and see the Twin Towers that King Kong had climbed carrying Jessica Lange. Everywhere I looked were apartment buildings like the ones Felix Unger and Oscar Madison lived in. To a kid so obsessed with pop culture, I'll admit, this was pretty darn cool. I found a cheap-looking deli, bought my first over-priced big city sandwich and headed back to work.

For the rest of the afternoon I continued to pore over Jack's old reports and at one point got brave enough to try my hand at the computer. This attempt went much better and I actually figured out how to get into the Lotus 1-2-3 program. The more I played around, the more I learned. I was beginning to almost feel like I knew what I was doing.

At some point in the afternoon, my phone rang. It was my new boss, Howard, calling to check in and see how I was making out on my first day. He said he was at some big paper conference, but the background sounds made it pretty obvious he was calling from a golf course. We could barely hear each other, so I had to keep talking louder and louder. He kept asking me questions I didn't know the answers to, so while I was floundering I was also screaming and starting to realize that I was causing a bit of a scene. My new neighbors, who had mostly ignored me so far, wanted to know what the hell the racket was. Their little heads kept popping up out of their cubicles like some office-based Whack-a-Mole game. I tried to ignore them and told Howard I was inputting numbers for the new budget report on the computer and that satisfied him enough to get him off the phone. He said he'd probably be back in the office by the end of the week. And that was that. Little did I know that that would be my last human interaction for the entirety of my first week of work.

When five o'clock came around, I sort of expected something to happen, someone to come check up on me, or someone to come tell me it was okay to go home. The day seemed to have lasted forever already, but I wasn't sure if it was okay for me to leave. I figured I'd stick it out as long as I could. By 5:06 I was out the door and headed to the subway. I still wasn't sure what I'd gotten myself into, but at least the first day was over.

Like I said, the rest of the week went by like I was alone on a desert island. Except I was surrounded by lots of people, who all seemed to be really busy. I nodded and smiled to everyone, and it's not like anyone was rude, but no one was going out of his or her way to be nice to the new kid. And I say "kid" because I was. I was twenty-two years old, and although I felt like a mature adult (as most twenty-two-year-olds do), I was still a pretty clueless kid. Especially compared to the world-weary publishing lifers surrounding me.

I did what I could to look busy and tried to figure stuff out on the computer, but the whole week dragged by interminably. My one friend in the whole building, Jack, was pretty tied up with his new gig. Worst of all, he was out of the office that Friday. I kind of was hoping the usual Friday Happy Hour would be different this week, since I was now firmly entrenched within the company, but without Jack around, no one really came by to invite me and I didn't have enough confidence to stroll in by myself and make friends. My first week of work ended exactly like my first day had, with me alone on the subway trying to figure out what the hell I'd done with my life.

8
ME AND BOB G.

That weekend, hanging out with my friends back in Connecticut, I of course bragged about how awesome my new job was. I didn't dare tell them I felt like some poor soul in a scientific study on human isolation. They didn't care what inner turmoil I was going through, they just wanted to hear cool stories about working at *Penthouse.*

The one thing everyone always wanted to know was if those *"Dear Penthouse"* letters were real. That question I could answer, not because of any first-hand knowledge at the time, but because when Jack started working at *Penthouse* that was the first question I had asked *him.* The truth is that the majority of the letters they printed *were* actual letters sent in by readers. The staff didn't write them. They were legitimate correspondence we received, opened, edited for grammar and published. Now were the events described in those letters true? I highly doubt it. In fact, years later one of the editors showed me the crates of letters they got in regularly and it was a little creepy. Many looked like they had been written by mental patients and serial killers. If you've ever seen the Unabomber manifesto, you have an idea of what these missives looked like. A lot of the return addresses I saw were prisons. But the letters were, for all intents and purposes, "real." The truly remarkable thing about all of the *"Dear Penthouse"* letters wasn't so much the content, but the fact that the magazine had ingeniously developed a way to get titillating editorial sent to them for free. Instead of paying a team of in-house writers to come up with erotic stories month after month, they had folks from all over the world clamoring for the chance to be featured in *Penthouse Magazine.* Free content was pouring in and it was the second most revered part of the magazine. *It was brilliant!*

My college buddies also wanted to know if I'd met Bob Guccione yet, or if I'd run into any of the *Penthouse* models in the hallway. I had not, but I made it seem like those encounters were imminent.

In fact, my real one-on-one exposure with Bob G. was still a few years down the road. As I struggled through my early days at *Penthouse,* I soon found out that Mr. Guccione almost NEVER came to the office. He worked every day from his home over on the East Side of town. I started in April of 1988 and the first time I saw Bob in the office was in February of 1990. Until then, the closest I would come to him is the huge picture that hung on the wall by my cubicle.

The entire office was decorated with huge blow-ups of covers, illustrations and photos from our magazines. The one I had to stare at everyday was a life-size shot of Bob G. in all his glory. He was sitting in an opulent chair staring intently at the camera. He wore a zippered denim top that was open halfway down his chest. A thick thatch of manly Italian chest hair peeked out. The guy oozed machismo. A shot of him alone staring at me everyday as I sat in my cubicle would have been menacing enough, but the other remarkable thing about the photo was that he had a naked woman sitting on his lap! She sat astride his left leg facing him, but was turned coquettishly towards the camera. Considering the fact that she was completely naked, it was not a raunchy shot. His hand was on her butt, covering most of her crack. The rest of the naughty bits, apart from a little side boob, were totally out of view. But there was no denying she was completely naked and sitting in Bob Guccione's lap.

They both kept vigil over me all day, every day. It was definitely strange, but I quickly got used to it. I assume lots of people work with pictures of their bosses staring down at them. Bank workers usually have the founder's portrait keeping tabs on them. Government employees usually have a picture of the president (their ultimate boss) peering down. But I don't think there were too many people sitting at their desk with a picture of their boss holding a naked lady staring at them every day.

POP CULTURE SIDE NOTE

The woman in the photo was Corinne Alphen. I knew this for a fact because just a few short years earlier when I was a high school senior I had developed a major crush on Miss Alphen after seeing her in the motion picture *Spring Break*. This flick was a typical teenage-boy movie that we would gravitate to every weekend. It wasn't good, but it had everything a teenage boy wants out of a flick: girls, beer and the occasional laugh. Miss Alphen was the lusty object of desire in the movie and her boobs, face, name and boobs were filed away in the alcove of my teenage boy brain. Yes, I know I said boobs twice, but that's only because they were such an extraordinary pair. I was, and still am, a pop culture trivia freak, so it wasn't that odd for me to remember the names and faces of people I saw in movies and on TV years earlier…to this day I can still name the entire cast of *Hogan's Heroes, The Bob Newhart Show* and every other show I watched as a kid. Here I was a few years later with a naked Corinne Alphen staring down at me. It was surreal. Deep down I knew she was looking down and mocking me from up there on Bob's knee, but there wasn't much I could do about it.

That's as close as I would get to Bob for quite a while. Guccione was just a mythical beast, not unlike Bigfoot, who was revered, but almost never seen. The real person at the top of the office food chain was Bob's longtime partner and soon-to-be wife, Kathy Keeton. Kathy had been one of his first employees when he'd started the magazine back in the sixties and they'd been together ever since. Bob was the founder and publisher; she was the president and chief operating officer. He was the dream-filled visionary and she was the tough-as-nails executive running the day-to-day operations. She was also, to put it quite simply, terrifying.

She was the bogeyman, Chupacabra and *loup-garou* all rolled into one. I was still years away from actually meeting her at this point, too, but her legend preceded her. I'd oft-heard Jack tell me tales of her anger and penchant for firing people on the spot. Even though I didn't really talk to that many people around the office yet, I had overheard enough conversations to get the sense that no one ever really wanted to cross paths with her.

Luckily, I was on the second floor and she was up on the third, so our worlds would seldom collide. Occasionally, however,

I would fall in harm's way and end up passing Kathy in the halls. She was quite a sight to behold. She walked like the former dancer she was, all straight posture, head held high. Which couldn't have been easy because she was always wearing the highest heels I've ever seen outside of porn. Plus, she happened to have a rather large bosom, which I assumed was artificially inflated since they never seemed to move in a way relative to gravity or common physics. They also rode a little higher on her carriage than one would expect for a woman her age. The other thing about her breasticular enhancements that was striking was how much she liked to put them out on display. No top was ever too sheer, no neckline too plunging. This may have just been the style at the time, and Kathy was certainly a fashion zealot, but I didn't know from fashion. All I knew was that she was the big boss and I feared those giant boobs like Superman feared Kryptonite.

In those early years, catching a glimpse of her down the hall sent me right into panic mode. I wasn't sure if I should smile amiably and say "Hi!" or just bow my head in deference and avoid eye contact. If possible, I would just avoid her altogether. If there was a water fountain nearby, I would quickly bury my face in it until the coast was clear. If there was an office within reach, I would duck in there with a phony question until she had moved on. In certain hallways, where no such escape presented itself, I would revert to my only option, turning tail and racing away Shaggy & Scooby-style like I'd just seen a g-g-g-ghost.

With her ridiculous cans always on proud display, I was never sure if they should be admired, avoided or ignored at all costs. Those giant breasts became the Medusa's stare of my entire *Penthouse* career. I was quite sure that if I ever looked directly at her headlights, I'd be tossed out of that office immediately by the sleepy, brown-suited security men doing their perpetual crossword puzzles in the lobby.

Fortunately, for most of us underlings, Kathy rarely left her opulently gaudy office on the third floor. But the one thing no one could ever escape was "the summons."

Throughout the office at that time we had an intercom system that was used to page people. This was before cell phones, email and instant messaging so the quickest way to get a hold of someone immediately was to have them paged to your extension. All day long you'd hear the speakers click on and inform someone, "Thomas Kreling, please call extension 518, Thomas Kreling, 518." Once I got used to these interruptions, I barely paid attention to them. I was almost always at my desk and few people ever needed to reach me, so I was never paged. Everyone else mostly ignored them as well. Except for the dreaded, "Please call extension 701." Whenever that number got announced, you could feel a chill go through the halls, if only for an instant. For that was Kathy's private line. Whoever was paged to extension 701, was being summoned up to Ms. Keeton's private lair. Immediately. It was like being called to the principal's office, except way worse.

As much as my hallway run-ins with her terrified me, I couldn't even fathom the fury that awaited those beckoned to call her immediately. Her office, or at least the idea of it at that point, always reminded me of Room 101 in George Orwell's *1984*—a place where everyone's worst fears come true.

Occasionally, someone wouldn't respond right away and would be paged a second time just a few minutes later. That would elicit an audible gasp from the cubicle crowd. The only thing worse than being summoned by the big boss was making the big boss wait.

It was widely known throughout the building that Kathy had a terrible temper and when you got on her bad side it was going to get ugly. She was a screamer too, and with her high-pitched South African accent it was quite alarming. I was merely in the vicinity of her office one day when she was chewing somebody out and the sound of her screeching coming through the walls was terrifying. Not everyone who got yelled at was fired on the spot, but it had to be a horribly deflating ordeal. One that I hoped to avoid at all costs.

Bob and Kathy were merely theoretical distractions in those early years and would not truly have an impact on me until later in my career. But I'm getting ahead of myself. I was heading into my second week on the job and I had bigger things to worry about.

9
Week Two

My second week started much differently than my first. I had
the commute down to a science by then, so the subway
didn't waylay me. And my boss was actually in the office. Howard
walked into my cube two seconds after I got there and wanted
to know how things were going. I stumbled a bit, tried to show
him the reports I'd started to put together on the computer and
did my best to not sound like an idiot. I don't think he was too
impressed, but at least he wasn't pissed. He asked if I'd placed the
paper orders for the month. I had not.

Here's the gist of what was one of the more important aspects
of my job. I was in charge of ordering all of the paper used to print
our magazines and manage said paper inventory. At the time we
were printing at least a dozen magazines a month, and *Penthouse*, by
far the biggest, used literally tons and tons of paper. At that point...
six days into my career in magazine publishing, I had no grasp of
the process. All I had to go on was Jack's five-minute explanation
from the week before. I really needed to figure this out quickly.

"So, did you get the orders in?" he asked again.

I didn't want to tell him I had been afraid to pull the trigger on the million-dollar orders and I didn't want to get Jack in trouble by saying he hadn't shown me the proper procedure. Finally, I explained to him that I had the preliminary orders together but was waiting to review them with Jack before actually placing them. My bluff worked. That answer was good enough and he went on his way.

I quickly called Jack and asked him for more help. He came downstairs and walked me through the process. Again. I don't know if Jack did a bad job of explaining the process or if I did a bad job of comprehending, but I could not quite figure out his system. I'll assume the trouble was all my fault because I really didn't know what I was doing. Or how magazines worked or really anything related to my job and the functions therein.

After he left, I was still rather confused. I went through the files for hours and finally of saw a kind of rhythm to the ordering process. Once I figured out what kind of paper was for each magazine, I realized that a lot of the orders placed were identical every month. So I just copied everything Jack had ordered the month before and called in all of the same orders. This involved calling the various paper salesmen they always used and verbally placing each order. I followed that up by typing up a purchase order, signing it and sending it out, one copy to the paper company, one upstairs to accounting and one for my file. By the end of that second Tuesday, all of my paper orders were in and I finally thought I had figured out my new job. My method of just doing exactly what Jack had done served me well. I took his budget reports from the file, which at the time were all handwritten, and input them into the computer. When new invoices came in, I just plugged in the new numbers, copied over Jack's variance descriptions and handed them in. Because they were neatly done on a computer and used all of Jack's terminology, Howard thought I was doing a good job.

I plugged away like this for a few weeks. When it was time to place paper orders again, I'd duplicate what I'd already done. I was starting to make friends with the paper guys over the phone. I made more friends around the office. But something still wasn't right.

I may have been adequately doing my job, but I was barely treading water. I felt like everything I did was wrapped in uncertainty. Day after day went by and my confidence level was draining. I wasn't really learning anything, I certainly wasn't getting ahead and the glitz and glamour of the job had literally dissolved on day one. Once again I found myself sitting on the train home late on a Friday night asking myself, *"Is this really what I want to do with my life?"*

10
CONSIDERING OTHER OPTIONS

Mindlessly repeating Jack's work day after day started making me feel mighty restless. I hadn't fully thought out taking this job and it was really starting to feel like I was heading down the wrong path. Maybe working in the city wasn't right for me. Or more appropriately, I wasn't quite ready to work in the big city. I was barely cutting it job-wise, and socially I was still a bit of a clueless outsider. I certainly didn't want to go back to my old job. Not only was I unhappy there to begin with, but I also didn't want to be seen as running back with my tail between my legs. So I set up an appointment with a headhunter in Stamford. I hoped that with my new, impressive-sounding publishing title, I would have my pick of jobs to choose from. Once again, I was wrong.

The woman was extremely nice and my job in New York publishing impressed her. Until she realized I'd only been there a month. She asked why I wanted to leave and I explained the craziness of the whole *Penthouse* scene and how nutty everyone was. What I'd hoped was a heart-to-heart amongst two seasoned business professionals was seen more as the petulant whining of an inexperienced kid in a job out of his league. She wasn't particularly overwhelmed by my personality, she thought my work experience and job history was all over the map and shot down whatever confidence I might have had quite quickly and easily. She laid it all out for me rather succinctly. "You're twenty-two years old, you don't have a college degree, you haven't stayed at any one job long enough to gain any real experience and you have a limited skill set. What do you think you're qualified to do?"

Unexpectedly knocked off my perch, I went with the usual interview answers about how my drive and dedication would make me a valuable asset in any position. Blah, blah, blah.

She raised her hand to stop me, took off her glasses and wearily rubbed her eyes. "Listen, I wouldn't even know what kind of job to try and send you in for. What's your long-range plan? What is it exactly you want to be doing?"

Excellent question. I had no idea. I didn't know what I wanted to do with my life. I just knew that to that point, I knew I hadn't come across it yet. The dull, glazed look on my face told her everything she needed to know.

I quickly went from someone who was wasting her time to someone who desperately needed help. She told me she wasn't going to recommend me for any jobs, but she strongly suggested I start figuring out what I wanted to do with my life. Her first recommendation was that I get my college degree and then seriously start looking at where I wanted to be five, ten years down the road. She wrapped up by saying, "You're actually lucky! A lot of people end up in jobs they hate for years and then try and switch career paths in their late twenties, which means starting over again from the bottom. At your age, you are in the perfect position to map out a game plan for your life and figure out where you want to go. Then you'll be in great shape!" I did not share her enthusiastic optimism.

In hindsight, what she said was one hundred percent on the money and exactly what I should have done. But at the time, all it felt like was that I had failed the interview and was still stuck in my confusing *Penthouse* position. I spent the rest of the weekend drinking beer and contemplating life. Mostly drinking beer.

My lack of a college degree was definitely a stumbling block. I had attended Fairfield University in Connecticut and was only a few courses shy of a diploma. Due to a lack of financial funds after getting as much support as I could from my folks, topping out my student loans and working endless part-time jobs, I stopped a semester shy of graduation to work full time. I then buried my head in the sand and hoped that jumping into the workforce full time would eradicate the need to earn those last few credits and get my degree. It seemed at first like my plan might be working—after all, I got the *Penthouse* job without a degree. But the chat with the headhunter was a wake-up call. Having that missing from my resume was only going to hurt me down the road.

I also assumed, probably correctly, that it would be harder to earn those credits, the older I got. I didn't really want to go back to class now, but it would be a lot easier to do at this stage in my life when most of my free time was devoted to beer and girls and the acquisition and appreciation of the those two things. If and when I ever became a real grown-up, I was pretty sure going to school part time would be even more of a drag. That's when I decided to take some part-time classes at the local satellite campus of the University of Connecticut.

Having figured out a solution to the degree part of the career equation, it was time to face the tougher question. What did I want to do for a living?

If all went according to plan I would soon have a college degree…in psychology. It seemed like a wise choice of major at the time, because those classes seemed the coolest to me, but now it was useless. I was never going to go into that field and it left me ill suited for anything in the real world. The only good thing was that I'd completed all the required courses for Psych, so I could finish up my credits with whatever electives I liked. Once again, I just had to figure out what I liked. And what I wanted to do. I had started to hate the guys I was living with. They all seemed so sure of themselves. They were my age, but they were all on paths that seemed right for them and they were all doing great. I was the idiot with night school brochures and a constant headache.

I hoped to take a night class that would at least get me closer to where I wanted to be, but since I didn't know where that was, I ended up just grabbing a class that I thought would be fun. It was a fiction writing class. I always enjoyed writing stories when I was growing up and had done reasonably well in all of the college writing courses I had taken, so figured I could bang this one out and not be too bored. I wish I could say that it was all part of a master plan to be a writer someday, but it just wasn't something I thought of doing. I didn't even think it was really a job you went for. I assumed all writers were great Hemingway/ Faulkner/Wolfe types with the urge to write coursing through their veins.

And through all of that, I was still stuck at *Penthouse*. But at least I was making moves. Maybe once I had a degree, I would be able to get a job somewhere better. For now, I was going to just have to struggle along and hopefully get better at my current job. And more importantly, maybe the job itself would get better.

11
HALF-DAY FRIDAYS!

One of the best things about that first year working in New York City was that the company had half-day Fridays in the summer. I was shocked; this was an odd publishing tradition that I was not expecting. From Memorial Day to Labor Day, the office closed at one o'clock every Friday. This was a thrilling bonus for the guy who sucked at his job and didn't really enjoy being there. The odd part was that as a commuter, it wasn't even all that much of a perk. If I left the office on a normal day at five o'clock, I could do the two-subway, train to Connecticut commute in ninety minutes. Not great timing but since it was rush hour things moved along smoothly.

On those summer Fridays, all bets were off. By the time I got down to Grand Central, I had to wait up to an hour for a train and then the local would often stop at Stamford, which meant having to jump on a shuttle bus to my nearby suburb. So the commute would run to almost three hours, door-to-door. On a half-day Friday, I was still home earlier than normal, but what a pain in the ass of a trip. What made it worse was that it was such a silly morning in the office anyway. No work ever got done. Few folks worked the traditional nine-to-five hours in the first place, so tons of people still strolled in after ten. The editorial folks were tied to the schedules of their magazines, so they did more time-shifting, working whole Fridays when the book was shipping and taking whole days off when not. Managers fell into two camps: those who worked Fridays as if nothing was different, maybe leaving at four o'clock once their underlings had departed, and those that flat-out didn't come in. My boss Howard was definitely in the second camp. Fridays were his special golf day, time to double down and play thirty-six. But like his other special golf times, he would never admit it. Every Thursday was the same routine, "See you tomorrow, Steve." Then he would call in from some golf course on Friday morning, make sure there were no emergencies and say he'd be stopping by the office after his "meeting." *Yeah, right.*

The rest of us fell into two camps as well, those who conscientiously strived to finish their workload so they could enjoy their time off and those of us who didn't really give a rat's ass. Guess which camp I was in? Most of my fellow stragglers would spend the morning making small talk, chatting about the weekend and wasting time until it was reasonably close enough to one o'clock to make our escape. I still didn't have a ton of friends there, but on Fridays everyone was in a happy mood so I was more likely to encounter a smiling face and actually hold down a conversation.

That half-Friday perk made the week much more bearable and added a lot more time to my social life. Knowing that Friday was a shortened cakewalk meant that Thursday nights were an all-out bacchanal. With no need to worry about suffering through a long full-day Friday, all I had to do was be semi-awake for a few hours and the day would be over quickly enough. Everyone in the company was in the same boat, so there were more Happy Hours, more parties and more socializing. It was the increased activity I needed to start connecting with my co-workers. And by the end of the summer, I actually started to feel like I almost fit in. I had a few friends, I was no longer the new kid and I knew my way around the city. Things were going well. Add in the fact that I was taking a night class on Mondays to get closer to my degree and I almost felt like I was heading in the right direction.

The worst part of summer Fridays was that they ended with that cold slap in the face of the first Friday after Labor Day. It was like the first day back at school when you're a kid after a long lazy summer. My body had grown so used to that four and a half day workweek that having to stay until five o'clock on a Friday was pure torture. Of course, I could just cut back on my Thursday night drinking and be normal again, but I was actually part of the crowd now. After spending so much time as an outsider, I certainly wasn't going to risk it by being a wet blanket on Thursdays. So I persevered. And learned to sleep on the train.

12
STEVIE'S FIRST BUSINESS TRIP

It may seem strange now, since kids seem to fly everywhere on vacation, but when I was twenty-two I had only been in an airplane twice. Once for a trip to Disney World when I was nine with my family, and once for an overnight trip to North Carolina my junior year of college to see my school team play in the first round of the NCAA tournament. On trip number one to Orlando in 1974, smoking was still allowed on planes and I got a tour of the cockpit and a set of pilot's wings that I cherished for years. On that second trip, I actually carried a plastic garbage bag with eight leftover beers through security and brought them all the way back to Connecticut. College kids do not like leaving beers behind. Now, my third airline trip beckoned.

My bosses sent me on a trip to our printing plant in Des Moines, Iowa, where I would attend a seminar they taught about the publishing arts. Since I was still living paycheck to paycheck, an all-expenses-paid business trip seemed very exciting. I was not going alone, however. They were also sending two young women from the *Penthouse* art department. They weren't that much older than I was, but were eons more mature. One of them was even married (the cute one). They lived in Manhattan and, listening to their conversation, I could tell that they had both traveled the world already. This being only my third trip to an airport, I already felt out of place. Especially after seeing their professional-traveler rolling luggage. I was schlepping around what could best be described as an enormous duffle bag. It looked less like luggage and more like that bag the guy in *Rear Window* used to carry his dead wife's body around in.

We flew out of LaGuardia Airport and I remember realizing pretty quickly that I should just keep my mouth shut and follow in the steps of my co-travelers. They were close friends at work and I'm sure weren't too thrilled about having to travel with Neophyte Jones the whole way. As I walked through the airport with them I can only imagine the pre-trip conversations they must have had about who their travel companion would be. "Maybe it will be that hunky guy from *Omni*? Or maybe that stud from ad sales?" Nope, it's just the dumbass kid from Connecticut with the sloppy fashion sense and bad hair.

They started out the trip in cranky moods. They were upset that they were being sent to Des Moines. They oozed that typical Manhattan attitude that going to Des Moines was somehow beneath them. I, on the other hand, was thrilled that I didn't have to pay for anything for three whole days.

While waiting for our flight, we found a table at the airport bar. The girls ordered martinis and I ordered a vodka on the rocks. (Side note: Jay McInerney's *Bright Lights, Big City* was a big highlight of my life at that point, and with my new big city job, I was trying to emulate the book's unnamed hero as much as possible. Mostly by drinking vodka on the rocks when I was trying to impress people. Further side note: I cannot handle vodka on the rocks.)

I was feeling pretty lubed-up by the time we boarded the plane. We had two more drinks on the two-hour flight into Chicago, then another on the shorter connecting flight into Des Moines. By the time we actually got to our destination, I was pretty snookered. I came to a very important decision about my two traveling companions. Mostly that the cute one was *really* cute. I knew she was married, but over the course of our travels, I could hear a lot of her confiding to the other one about how things weren't going so great at home. The other thing that became evident was that I had gone from being the shy follower at the beginning of our trip and turned into Mr. Sociable. I think the ladies actually appreciated me coming out of my shell at some point as we flew over Pennsylvania and Ohio, but by the time we were waiting for our shuttle bus to the hotel they had already grown bored of my shtick. In their defense, I didn't have a whole lot of socializing skills back then and I have no doubt that my blathering grew boring and bothersome rather quickly. I hadn't really lived any kind of life yet, so I rambled on about sports, Tom Wolfe's *Bonfire of the Vanities* (which I had just finished reading and I thought made me sound educated), and when in doubt I always had my old standby, random '80s movies and '70s sitcoms.

When we got to the hotel, a lovely Holiday Inn somewhere in Des Moines, we checked in and they quickly peeled off to their rooms. When I suggested we explore the town a bit and go find something to eat, they said they were exhausted and I was quickly on my own. The first thing I did was look for the room service menu. I drunkenly ordered a small feast for myself and settled in to watch some *Monday Night Baseball* on ABC. This was long before baseball was broadcast nationally, so I was happy to watch the Pirates face off against the Reds. Soon my dinner arrived. I don't even know if Holiday Inns still do room service, but in 1988 in Des Moines, Iowa, they did it pretty well. The guy who brought in all that food was a little surprised to find only one person in the room. He quickly took away two of the three place settings he'd brought and set up my overwhelming repast. There were two shrimp cocktails, a deluxe burger platter, a double side of onion rings and a Chocolate Lava Cake for two. Along with two Dr. Peppers. The vodkas had taken their toll and I wanted to avoid any more booze.

I ate, drank and was merry watching my baseball game and wondering what the next day held for me. I had never been to a seminar before. I had been a pretty lazy student a few years earlier, but now that I was being paid to learn, I was hoping things would be different. As I polished off the last of my buffet for one, I was feeling pretty good about myself. I was now a grown-up with a real job, who went on business trips and ate room service and traveled with attractive girls. That's when I looked out my window for the first time and saw my co-workers sitting in the hotel's atrium. They had just finished a nice dinner and were laughing it up together having a grand old time. So they weren't really all that tired after all. They were simply tired of me. And just like that, I felt like an outsider again. I was that shy little boy without any friends. Except now I was alone in a hotel room. In Iowa. *Sigh!*

The next day was spent in a cramped conference room with representatives from a bunch of other magazines all being taught the basics of magazine printing and production. There was a *Guns & Ammo* guy there, a few folks from *Cat Fancy*. Lots of people from craft magazines (who knew people needed so many periodicals about knitting?). And then us, the three representatives from

Penthouse Magazine. People always had unrealistic expectations when meeting *Penthouse* employees (although I can't say I blamed them because I had the same notions before I started working there). They expected anyone from our magazine to be an impossibly buxom woman in a nightie. So they were always disappointed when they encountered me. Now they had three disappointments. Me, my plainish compatriot and the cute one, who although she was cute, could never match the "luscious model" expectations of our fellow attendees. Once they got over their disappointment, we all settled down to learn.

That two-day course was probably the best thing I could have done for my career. I learned a lot about what my actual job entailed. It was all stuff I probably should have been taught by my boss during that first week on the job, but wasn't. Between trying to figure things out on my own in New York and actually seeing the process here in Iowa, I was starting to get a grasp of what it is my job entailed and how to do it. As an added bonus, I started making friends with the Iowa printing plant folks. While my naiveté didn't play out all that well to city-dwelling twentysomethings back in Manhattan, I fit right in with the good people of Des Moines. So we drank beer, told stories and bonded for a few days and I almost felt like I belonged. And with the newfound knowledge of what I was actually supposed to do back at the office, I was feeling on top of the world.

After a wrap-up dinner at the conference where we all had a lot to drink, the three of us from *Penthouse* went back to our hotel. We said good night and I went to my room. I packed my bags for the early morning departure and debated ordering up a room service snack or maybe even venturing down to the hotel bar for one last beer. Since this was the end of my expense account adventure, I wanted one last little treat before bed. I wandered over to the window and saw my cute traveling companion sitting alone outside of her room. She looked rather sad as she sipped her beer and smoked her cigarette. Basking in confidence after a successful couple of days, I decided to venture out. *What I was going to do?* I don't even know. I had no finesse with women, but if she were single I would have tried to at least make a move. But she was married. Not happily married, but married. I knew she was angry with her husband from listening in on her conversations. Was she angry enough to cheat on him? Was I the type of guy who wanted to hit on a married woman? I stood there trying to figure out what to do, when I realized that the absolute worst scenario was to be caught staring at her silently from my window.

I gathered up my nerve, checked my breath and ventured out. Like I said, I don't have any game, but whatever I was thinking must have been quite evident from the way I sauntered over to her. She looked up at me and I saw that she had obviously just been crying. Before I could even ask if she wanted me to grab us a few drinks, she looked at me and said, "Go back to your room, Stephen." This comely lass reprimanded me like a grade school principal and sent me on my way. I turned tail and disappeared. I went out there high on a few days of misplaced confidence and got sent away like a kid caught with his hand in the cookie jar. As cocksure as I was feeling moments before, I was quickly put back in my place. I was still just a little boy in a grown-up world.

I drunkenly drifted off to sleep. I shook off the cute girl's rebuttal by telling myself how much better life back at the office was going to be now that I actually learned more about the biz. The next Monday morning I strolled into the office chock-full of confidence. That's when I found out that I had almost bankrupted the company.

13
HOW I MISSPENT MILLIONS OF DOLLARS

It seems that while I thought my paper-ordering process was going swimmingly, it was in fact going terribly, horrifically wrong. This became apparent to me the morning Howard, his boss the Cheeky Brit, and some guy from accounting all bounded into my cubicle with a full head of steam. Howard started firing questions at me, then the Brit started yelling at me and the accountant started showing me all sorts of computer printouts that made absolutely no sense to me. I stared back at them silently with a dull-eyed look of confusion. All I knew for sure was that I was in a deep load of shit.

It seems that during the first time I'd placed the orders, many things had gone awry. All of them my fault. I'd somehow ordered twice as much paper that first month than we actually needed. I'm still not sure how it happened, but it did. Ordering twice as much paper as you need, at those volumes, was a BIG problem. But it would have been salvageable if caught quickly. It was not. I had repeated the same mistake for *four straight months*. No wonder the paper salesmen were so chummy with me over the phone! They'd all achieved their quota for the year in just a few months. I had no idea what was going on. I was just a dopey kid in a cubicle, scratching out purchase orders, signing my name and filing the documents away. It should have been my first hint to the lunacy of the company that they had absolutely no checks and balances in place to stop one person (a stupid new employee of all things!) from having the power to spend that much money.

A QUICK PRIMER ON MAGAZINE PAPER

The paper used in the massive printing plants comes in enormous rolls that are three feet high and as wide around as a shower stall. Little did I know that I was ordering hundreds of tons of these rolls a month. What were just numbers on an order form to me, filled endless trucks and train cars throughout the country. While I sat cluelessly playing Minesweeper on my computer, several paper plants were working extra shifts to meet my purchasing demands. Men were working overtime. Trucks were driving through the night. Train cars were being filled to capacity. And I had no clue. The paper just kept pouring into our printing plant in Des Moines.

The goal is to ship in only the paper you need as close to the printing date as possible so as to not have to pay the plant to store it for you. My first month's orders came in and there was a ton of overage, so they stored it. Then the second month's orders came in and they stored that, too. By the time my fourth month's orders came in, they had literally run out of places to put my paper. It was scattered throughout warehouses all over Iowa. That's what triggered the avalanche of crap that I was now in. The accountant had gotten the fee for all of the excess storage and had been confused. Then they discovered that I had bought almost a year's worth of paper in just four short months. Millions and millions of dollars more than we needed. All purchased by a kid who could barely afford the hot-dog lunches he was buying himself at Gray's Papaya on 72nd Street.

———

So there I was, getting yelled at by all three of them. They were desperate for an explanation. What the hell had I done?!! And truly, I had no idea. I assumed I was going to be fired on the spot. After not getting an answer out of me, other than sputtering, blathering sighs of confusion, they left. I was alone in my cubicle, my heart beating like a jackrabbit. Nosy folks from my area kept poking their head in after all the fireworks to see what was going on, but I shooed them away as if I was trying to fix the problem. In reality, I was trying my best not to cry and wondering what the hell I was going to do without a job. I could barely afford rent as it was—what was going to happen to me when they threw me out on my ass?

At least an hour went by and I barely moved. I assumed someone from Security would be by at any minute to escort me out of the building. But they never came. After a while, Howard came over and told me to come to his office. As scared as I was walking in there, I realized something. Howard looked exactly like I did. Scared. I didn't realize it at first, but here's what I think happened. I had fucked up. Royally. But Howard was the one who had hired me, and at the end of the day, he was the one responsible. And

Howard's boss, the Cheeky Brit, oversaw the whole production department, so he was ultimately responsible. And he reported to the CFO and ultimately Bob, himself. So he was in a shitload of trouble, too. Not even the accountant was in the clear. At some point someone should have noticed the millions of dollars I was spending and raised a red flag much earlier in the debacle. Everyone had dropped the ball in this little escapade. So they decided to do what all great leaders do, sweep it under the rug.

Firing me might have been the obvious solution, but it wouldn't really solve anything. Instead they read me the riot act and told me to make things right. The good thing about paper is that it doesn't really go bad. We would be able to use it eventually. We would just have to pay for storing it. Somehow the Cheeky Brit worked it out with his printing plant cronies that we wouldn't have to pay full boat for the storage. The accountant worked out payment schedules for the orders and floated some of it on the balance sheet so it didn't fiscally destroy the company. And Howard smoothed things over with the paper guys. They weren't too happy to hear that we wouldn't be placing any orders for a while until we burned through our massive inventory, but they were smart enough to accommodate one of their biggest customers.

And me? *I couldn't believe I still had a job.* No one wanted to fire me because that would make them look bad for hiring me in the first place. I was so relieved that I actually became doubly determined to *really* learn what the hell I was doing. I pestered Jack endlessly about how things were supposed to be done. I went to more training seminars at the printing plant, I toured paper mills, I improved my computer skills and, most importantly, I figured out how to manage a paper inventory and actually kept track of every single roll I ordered. I would go to the plant in

Des Moines regularly to keep tabs of my handiwork. Their paper warehouse looked like the government depot they stored the Ark of the Covenant in at the end of *Raiders of the Lost Ark*, except it was filled with my poorly ordered inventory. Rolls of paper were stacked two stories high as far as the eye could see and I was the idiot crawling around on top of the shaky, mouse-dropping-covered bundles doing the physical inventory. Eventually, we finally used all of the excess paper I had ordered and got back into the appropriate rhythm of things. My job was safe again. For now.

14
PERSONAL LIFE?

When I would meet people for the first time and tell them I worked at *Penthouse*, they would always have one of two reactions. If it was a guy, it was always a version of "No way! That's so cool! What's it like? Do you meet the models?!" And of course, as I mentioned earlier, the endless questions about if the letters to *Penthouse Forum* were real or not. I'm serious, this must be the most important question in the history of the world. Every dude wanted to know. It's kind of like when a kid finally starts asking if Santa Claus is real or not. If they're asking the question they probably know the actual truth, but part of them is desperate to hang on to the dream.

When women found out where I worked, it was usually a much more subdued reaction, "Oh. That's...interesting." I could see that they were trying to make sense of it in their heads. On paper, I had a decent job at large international magazine publisher, but to a lot of women it sounded like the equivalent of working the door at a strip club.

So my dating life took a bit of a downturn. I wasn't exactly lighting up the scoreboard before that, but I really hit a dry spell once girls found out I spent my day with pictures of naked women everywhere. The few that were okay with what I did quickly turned out to not be the types I was interested in. Quite the conundrum.

On a corporate level, the name *Penthouse* was scaring off folks as much as it was scaring away girls for me on a personal level. That's when they made the move to change the name of our parent company to General Media International. They couldn't have come up with a more generic name, but it was perfect. GMI, as we were now called, was a much more innocuous name for a company. People in the industry still knew who we were, but it was like having a secret code word. Advertisers no longer had to say they were going to drinks with the *Penthouse* guys; it was simply a GMI meeting. The same went for all of the outside folks who may not have relished having *Penthouse* as a client, but had no problem listing GMI as a big customer. I wish I could say it also helped me with the ladies when my business cards now said GMI instead of *Penthouse*, but it did not. I was still a lonely, lovelorn young man.

With all of the after-hours socializing that everyone in the company did, it was pretty common for inter-office hook-ups to occur. And that made a lot of sense, especially once I saw how hard it was to meet someone outside of our crew. Even though the owner of the company and its president had been an item for decades, inter-office relationships were frowned upon. Howard had called me into his office early in my career, when he'd first seen me flirting with someone at the office, and gave me a very stern warning, about "dipping my pen in company ink." A warning that would have been much easier to heed had I not found out a few months later that he was diddling one of the ladies up on the third floor. They made for quite the couple, he being short and rather round and she being tall and thin. The one thing they had in common was their shared love of cigarettes, which left them both with a similar ashen pallor. I assume during their taboo out-of-the-office trysts, they lit up their Marlboros before, during and after the main event.

I resisted the siren song of the inter-office dalliance, since I quickly learned that that is not the best course of action. When things go wrong in a relationship, the last thing you want is to have to pass by that person in the hall everyday. And with all of the inbreeding going on in that place, you could read a lot into all of the awkward head nods and unreturned greetings that happened over the course of a day.

As much as I resisted the urge to go after anyone at the office, there was one encounter during this time that had quite the opposite effect. It involved one of my co-workers in the production department who we secretly referred to as the Muffin Lady. She was nice enough. She was one of those women who always had pictures of her nephews and her cats plastered all over her cubicle. I didn't know it at the time, but I've encountered endless variations of this personality over the years. The cats and the nieces and nephews they talk about as if they were their own are a telltale sign that they are missing something in their own lives. It was further evidenced by the constant baking of treats for co-workers as a way to ingratiate herself and be appreciated (thus the nickname). But at the time, she was just a nice co-worker. She talked to me and that made her okay in my book.

One Friday night after yet another Happy Hour with a ton of folks from the office, as often happens, the huge crowd dwindled down to just a handful of us. It was me, my buddy Jack, a few of his friends from the advertising department and the Muffin Lady. We were headed to another bar when someone suggested we go up to two of the girls' nearby apartment. I filled my usual role as amiable follower/lemming. My only slight concern was that it was getting late and Jack and I had to start thinking about getting to Grand Central for the late-night train ride home. But popping up for one quick drink couldn't hurt, could it?

Once we got to the apartment and everyone got a drink, I realized the dynamic of the group I was now in. It was three guys and three girls. Jack's buddy, Jesse, and one of the girls hung out with us in the living room for about two minutes before retiring to a back bedroom amorously. I turned to Jack to comment about the relations that were about to happen in that back room, when I realized that Jack was now making out with the other girl.

"Wait, what the hell is going on here? Was this a double room-mate hook-up?" I thought to myself. It was. Jesse was in a bedroom with one girl and now the other girl was leading Jack to a second bedroom. Jack was less of a cocksman than me, so this was wholly unexpected. Then I realized that their departure meant it was just the Muffin Lady and me.

Unsure what to do as we both sat there on the couch, I laughed about this surprising turn of events going on in the back rooms and grabbed the TV remote. I figured we'd just hang out, drink our beers and watch some tube. Muffin Lady had other ideas. She snuggled up on the couch next to me. *Uh-oh.* She wasn't unattractive by any means and, like I said, she was perfectly nice, but I had zero interest in her sexually. We were probably more compatible looks-wise than I would have admitted back then, but I still wasn't feeling it. As I surfed the channels, I could feel her staring at me, waiting for me to make a move. I have no moves, so even if I was interested in taking things to the next level, I don't know what I would have done.

So there we were, in a stalemate. She stared at me while I stared just as intently at the TV screen across the room, checking channel after channel. At some point I stumbled upon the infamous *Robin Bird Show* on public access and naked people filled the screen. I almost squealed in fear. I jammed the remote's button again and luckily ended up on *Nick at Nite*. It was an old episode of *Welcome Back Kotter*. I mumbled something about loving this show and put all my attention to following the Sweathog hi-jinks. Muffin Lady carried on undeterred. She nuzzled in closer. Then she started caressing my face. No one before or since has ever caressed my face. Who does that? Other than maybe a doctor checking for swollen glands. After an entire *Kotter* episode of face caressing, I heard a door open. I hoped it was Jack ready to go home. It wasn't. It was just one of the girls running out to use the bathroom. A minute later she scampered back to her room. It was enough of a distraction that Muffin Lady stopped petting my face. But once the bedroom door shut, I was once again on my own.

As Muffin Lady turned back to me, I did the only thing left at my disposal; I pretended to be asleep. Sitting up. She caressed my face a little bit more and even tried nuzzling my ear. I clamped my eyes shut tight and pretended to be passed out cold. It's the same thing I would have done if I'd come face to face with a grizzly bear in the middle of the woods. And she reacted much I like I think the puzzled grizzly would have. The nuzzling stopped, but I could still feel her sitting next to me. *Was she still staring at me? Christ, this was weird!* After another long, silent stretch, I suddenly felt her hand caressing my inner thigh. Now, even though I wasn't attracted to her, this is a move that would make even the devoutest monk consider surrender. If she persisted, my ruse was going to be discovered and then I'd have quite the dilemma on my hands, or more appropriately, in hers. Luckily the huge number of beers imbibed earlier and the fact that she gave up rather easily, allowed me to continue my sleepy subterfuge.

Frustrated and bored, she eventually lost interest altogether and I heard her gather her things and slip out the door of the apartment. Like a stowaway not wanting to be discovered, I still pretended to be asleep for five more minutes before finally opening my eyes to make sure the coast was clear. I was now alone in the empty room. A quick glance at the clock and I realized that the last train out was leaving in fifteen minutes. What to do? Do I go knock on the door and tell Jack we should leave? If I were on the other side of that door, I would certainly NOT want to be interrupted. Do I just bolt and try to get home on my own? I was still relatively new to the city at that point and usually just followed Jack around. I didn't think I was ready for the solo dash to Grand Central at 4:00 AM. New York City was still a bit of a scary place in the late '80s. Especially for a drunk, dopey kid from the suburbs. So I did what I do best. Nothing. I got comfortable on the couch, closed my eyes and drifted off to the sounds of Kotter once again being yelled at by Mr. Woodman. Three or four hours later, Jack roused me from my slumber and we slunk off into the early morning light to take the 7:00 AM train back to Connecticut.

Come Monday morning, the Muffin Lady acted like nothing ever happened. And I made sure to never be left alone with her again.

15
THE GOOCH!

Up to this point in my career at *Penthouse*, I still had yet to meet the man himself, Bob Guccione, or "the Gooch" as he was often called. The closest I'd come was listening to him make his occasional appearances on *The Howard Stern Show*. I'd sit in my cubicle listening to that velvety baritone promoting the latest issue and I almost felt like I was part of something important. I know, it was just pictures of naked ladies, but we sold millions of copies and I was part of it. It was towards the end of my second year at the company when I actually saw the Gooch in the flesh. It was a rare sighting indeed, because not only was he out of his mansion, but this compulsive night owl was actually out before noon. The special event that had gotten Bob out in the morning daylight was the funeral of Malcolm Forbes, which Bob and Kathy attended. Afterward he came to the office and, among other stops, popped into the office of the Cheeky Brit to see how things were going.

When I'd heard he was in there I quickly grabbed a folder and headed over there trying to think of some pretense to pop in and actually meet the man, the myth, the icon. I was not alone. A bunch of other folks had the same idea and were milling about the halls and cubicles around the Brit's office. I did not get a chance to actually meet him, but I heard him. Bob's voice was his most distinctive feature; it was a rich, deep baritone that lent an air of gravitas to everything he said. It was the kind of voice you follow into battle. The voice of a leader that made you WANT to be a follower. At the time he was still one of the richest men in the country and a publishing legend. He did acknowledge all of us minions on his way out, told us to keep up the good work and then he was gone. Other than the occasional Christmas party sighting from afar, that would be as close as I would get to meeting the big guy until he extended his hand and introduced himself to me when I sat at his dining room table four years later.

16
THE BOSSES OF ME

While neither Mr. Guccione nor Ms. Keeton was an integral part of my life yet, Howard and the Cheeky Brit certainly were.

Howard Hobner, in addition to not firing me for the screw-ups I had early on, genuinely seemed to want me to do well. I'm sure most of that was because the better I did my job, the easier his was. Howard had one great move that was an endless source of humor to me. He was a degenerate golfer. Despite his short, stout nature, he was actually pretty good, a single-digit handicap if I remember correctly. So from the first warm days of March to the blustery early days of November, Howard would play a lot of golf, during the week, instead of being at the office. Every time, he'd do the same thing; he'd pop over to my cubicle and tell me he had an important meeting to go to outside of the office but he should be back around five. At the beginning, that possible return "around five" kept me glued to my chair. Even though he was gone, I didn't want to sneak out early only to have him come back to the office at 4:45 and find I was already gone for the day. But of course, he never came back.

I would sit there staring at the clock until the needle hit 5:00 PM and then I'd bolt for the door. After a few months, I started to sense a pattern and asked Jack about it. He just laughed and said Howard had never come back to the office the whole time he'd worked for him. At first I felt a little insulted that I was being played like that. Then I realized that it just meant I had no one looking over my shoulder most afternoons. It got to the point that I started covering for his absences since I really didn't want him to get in trouble because then he'd start being around more.

In his absence, I did try to have a little fun with him. I would go into his office and change his speed dial numbers. So when he'd come in the next morning and try to call our printer, he'd end up connected to a gay Spanish phone sex line. The fact that he always used his speakerphone delighted me to no end. You'd just hear him make the call and then, "*Hola chico grande, ¿Cuál es su placer sucio?*" He'd curse and hang up, and sometimes try again. If it wasn't a phone sex line, it was a radio station or even just a nearby deli. Anything to get him to curse at his phone. Once I changed his speed dial to call his second line so that as soon as he dialed, his other line would ring, so he'd hang up and answer it, only to find dead air at the end. He would get caught in this loop for a while before the cursing would begin. Not the most mature move on my part, but it brought a little levity, at least to my day.

While Howard was nice and all, it was the Cheeky Brit that I looked up to. I dug this guy, I really did. And I can confidently say it was one hundred percent because of his British background. I don't know what my deal is, I have a Brit fixation. Maybe it's because I was born during the British invasion. Maybe my ancestors were raped and pillaged by the Redcoats during the Revolutionary War. Maybe my really old (alien) ancestors crash-landed in Bath and created Stonehenge. I've always tended to dig anything having to her Majesty's realm. I loved Dick Van Dyke's cockney chimney sweep in *Mary Poppins*, Richard Dawson's Newkirk on *Hogan's Heroes* and the cherished works of the late, great Benny Hill. The Beatles were omnipresent in my youth, quickly followed by a slavish devotion to The Stones and The Who. And of course there was the nanny from *The Nanny and the Professor*, Juliet Mills. She played Nanny Phoebe Figalilly and with her golden tresses and sly accent, she got this young TV viewer's heart a-racing in ways I'd never experienced before. I was the king of TV reruns in the early '70s and Nanny Figalilly was the first member of my TV crush club that would eventually include Wrangler Jane, Ellie Mae Clampett and later, Pinky Tuscadero. But Figallily was my first and that soft British lilt still holds a place in my heart.

The Cheeky Brit was my first encounter with a true Englishman, but he was no James Bond type. He was more along the Monty Python spectrum. He had a cheeky sense of humor (thus the name) and for some reason he liked me, which is always the easiest way to get me to like you back. I'm not very exclusionary. I live by the perpetual Golden Rule of childhood: You like me? I like you. We both like pizza and baseball? Awesome! Let's be best friends.

I couldn't tell you why the Cheeky Brit liked me, I was still the newborn foal of the publishing world, scrambling about on shaky legs and ill-fitting grown-up clothes, but he cut me a lot of slack. He let me sit in on a lot of meetings that I probably didn't deserve to be at, but I certainly learned from them. Those meetings allowed me to be a fly on the wall and see how things ran. I heard and oversaw many decisions made about what would go in the magazine, what pieces couldn't run because of legal issues, how they dealt with Bob. The most important thing I learned from these meetings was not to be intimidated by executives. It quickly became apparent that the people with the best titles weren't always the smartest people in the room and that sometimes just how you manage relationships with people allows you to do precisely what you want. I watched the Cheeky Brit manipulate people and get his way more often than I can remember. He did it with charm, flattery and no small amount of bullshit. A skill set which I tried to copy at the time and still use to this day.

17
THE *PENTHOUSE* PEEPS

In addition to some of the folks I've already discussed, the place was awash with other quirky characters. I know I wasn't the most normal guy in the world, but I felt pretty darn sane sitting in my cubicle in the middle of this island of misfit toys that made up the rest of the staff.

One of the first oddballs I encountered was Civil War Todd. He was a nebbishy-looking guy who sat in the office closest to my cubicle. I didn't really understand what he did. It had something to do with *Omni,* our science magazine, and a few other titles he always referenced, but I knew we hadn't produced in years. He was not a regular nine-to-fiver, he would stroll in late, leave early, be there for ten hours a day for a whole week or not be seen for days at a time. Occasionally people would come looking for him and since I was the closest warm body, they would ask if I knew where he was. I was usually clueless, but told them to make sure to knock on the door because even when he was there, he would close his office door to work. There was a rumor going around that a mailroom guy had once walked in and caught him pleasuring himself at his desk, but I never got true confirmation on that. It wouldn't surprise me if it was true. He looked like the kind of guy you would think would get caught pleasuring himself in his office.

At some point during my first month, Todd realized that someone new was sitting in my cubicle and came over to introduce himself. Not too many folks did that when I first started so I was happy to have an actual person to talk to. For the first five minutes. Then it got ugly. Todd was a Civil War reenactor. I knew very little about the Civil War and even less about reenacting it, but Todd went on for close to an hour about how hardcore he was in the reenacting scene. As he droned on, unaware of his audience of one's waning interest in the subject matter, I longed for the days of just sitting in my cubicle being ignored by everyone. Eventually, after covering most of the great North-South battles, from Sumter to Appomattox, he grew weary and retired to his office. I made a mental note to avoid any further conversation with him. For the rest of my life.

Since I was tall and could see over the maze of cubicles, I became pretty good at avoiding people by recognizing the tops of their heads over the fabric covered walls. Which is how I had my second encounter with Todd. On the other side of my bank of cubicles was the production office. It was a large, well-lit room with a huge, waist-high table in the center that they used to look at all the magazine proofs that came in. It also doubled as a communal meeting spot for the production department for announcements, birthday parties, etc. This was also the home base of the aforementioned Muffin Lady. Every Friday she would come in with a lovely basket of homemade muffins. They were always tasty and she left them out for all to partake. All she asked was that you drop a quarter or two into the nearby jar to help offset the cost of the ingredients. It wasn't a moneymaking scheme. The woman enjoyed baking and if she could do it and provide tasty treats for her co-workers at no cost to herself, she was game.

One Friday I stood up to see Todd running out of the production room in a hurry, huddled over like he was carrying something. As was habit by that time, as soon as I saw him coming, I ducked away inside my cubicle, unseen. As he hustled passed me, I could see what he was holding. He had over a half-dozen muffins piled in his two cupped hands. He quickly made the turn and disappeared into his office and closed the door.

Intrigued, I wandered over to the production office where a few other department members were wandering back in after a staff meeting. The Muffin Lady wandered over to her basket and cursed. All of her muffins were gone and almost no money was in the cup. She loudly complained that people were all scavengers and vowed to never make muffins for them again. I wanted to explain that it wasn't a bunch of people who were taking advantage of her generosity, but one odd duck of a co-worker who had stolen a handful of muffins. I thought about speaking up, but realized it wasn't really a skirmish I wanted to get in the middle of, much like the aforementioned Battle of Fort Sumter. Especially since Todd was an incessant bore and I'd already had my one uncomfortable encounter with the Muffin Lady. For those of you keeping score at home, she was the young woman who so oddly caressed my face that one strange night just a few months before.

The case of the missing muffins would have finally given our crack security team something to work on. Ever since I'd seen the security guard's gun on that first day, I'd been studying the squad of ex-cops that protected us everyday. The lobby had two armed guards, checking IDs and announcing visitors. Then each floor had its own armed guy sitting at a table in front of the elevator banks. Were they there to protect the employees within or to guard against somebody walking off with a fax machine? (*Don't laugh, they were expensive back then!*) The truth is they were all there to make Kathy feel safe. Whether she needed it or not, I'll never know, but she wanted it and that was all that mattered. That was the important lesson to learn, whatever Bob and Kathy wanted, they got, and we just had to make everything else work around them. Truthfully, they ran the company and *should* have been entitled to whatever they wanted.

So that's why we had an entire security force, attired in khaki polyester slacks and dark brown poly-blend blazers. We paid for their uniforms, their bullets and their firing range time. And in turn, Kathy felt protected 24/7. The security force she saw was not the same one the rest of us saw. They were a decent bunch of guys, but they knew how to game the system. I loved shooting the shit with them. If there's one thing about ex-cops, they know how to tell a good story. And they were a pretty laid-back bunch. The only real annoying thing about them was that they all reeked of smoke. You could still smoke cigarettes in offices back in those days and these guys didn't miss a beat. They chain-smoked the day away. I can't imagine they had more than one or two of those brown blazers with the *Penthouse* logo embroidered on the chest, and its not like they got them dry-cleaned every night, so as soon as I would get within ten feet of one of these guys I could smell the stench of stale cigarettes from the past ten years. It was a real treat. There they would sit, day after day, and do their crossword puzzles, study *The Racing Form*, run the office gambling pools; doing whatever they could to stave off the boredom of sitting in the same spot for eight hours a day trying to stay awake. On many occasions, I'd pass by a slumped-over guard sound asleep at his station. In his brown jacket he looked not unlike a hibernating bear cub with a severe nicotine addiction. But these laid-back guys were not the fearsome security experts Kathy saw.

Kathy would always be driven over to the office from their fancy joint on the Upper East Side. Obviously, the security guys at the front door would get the heads-up when her arrival was imminent. Jackets were straightened, counters were cleared, and the lobby was neatened. She strolled in past held doors and made her way upstairs. The third floor guard already had the heads-up, so crosswords were hidden, cigarettes extinguished and he sat at the ready. As soon as the elevator doors opened he would jump up with a quick, "Good morning, Miss Keeton!" Another door was opened for her and she headed to her inner sanctum, and everybody was taken off high alert and relaxed. The same process occurred whenever she left the building so that she only saw everyone at his or her best. I'm sure that's how it works at a lot of companies, but it was just so comical to see it in action.

The security guard on the second floor eventually became a very important part of my life. His name was Salvatore and he was the same guy who was working at the front desk when I first came to interview for the job. We ended up becoming pals over the years and at some point he let it be known that he was also a part-time bookmaker. At the time I was gambling through another college buddy, but it was a third-party connection and sometimes my bets didn't make it in, or the guy would say he never got the message. Now I had Sal offering up his services. I wasn't even a big-time player at that time, maybe I'd bet fifteen or twenty bucks on games, but Sal was at my beck and call. I could call him minutes before any game and get a full assortment of lines and spreads.

It cracked me up that this ex-cop was running an illicit gambling operation. We didn't really talk about it too much at the office for obvious reasons, but everyone knew about Sal's side business. I had a special phone number to call whenever I wanted to bet. I never asked him, but from the sound of things it seemed like he was sitting in a small room, at tables with a bunch of other bookies all working the phones. I'm not sure why I had that picture in my head. Maybe I saw the movie *The Sting* too many times as a kid. I would call my special line and if someone other than Sal answered I had to ask for him by his special codename, "Champ." I'm not sure what Champ's home life was like, but I do know that for years whenever I dialed that line, Champ was waiting at the other end, surrounded by the din of other bookies on other phones having the same conversation.

As much as they stunk of smoke, I could have used one of those security guys one night when I had my first run-in with one of the original employees of the company. He was another Brit at the company who I saw quite often, only because his window office was near to where I sat. I thought of him as the non-cheeky Brit. He was a legend in the organization. He was one of the original guys sitting around Bob's kitchen table back in the day when the magazine had been created and had been part of the business ever since. He was a nice-enough Brit, who mostly kept to himself. He'd stroll in late, work in his office for a bit, then go out for an extended liquid lunch, then come back and play classical music extremely loudly in his office. He was what you would call a real character. I sat twenty feet away from him for two years, and I don't think he ever knew I existed. I can't blame him, I was very unmemorable at the time (*some say I still am*). He'd been anchored in at *Penthouse* for over twenty years and I'm sure he'd long ago stopped remembering the names of the little folk who passed through these halls on their way to bigger and better things. At the random times we would be with the same crowd at some Happy Hour or event, I always enjoyed listening to his storytelling about the old days. I've always been a sucker for a British raconteur, and still am.

But my most vivid memory of him was in 1990, just a few weeks after the Berlin Wall came down. We were all out at some drunken get-together and he was going off on some political tangent that I could barely follow, but it seemed to be about how stupid and insufferable we Americans are when it came to world politics. I'm sure I didn't argue, because as a twenty-four-year-old drunk living in New York, I was wildly out of touch with just about everything happening outside of Manhattan's twelve square miles. But he needed someone to argue with and he landed on me.

"All of you are making such a big deal out of bringing down the Berlin Wall!!" he yelled at me. In my defense, I could have cared less about the Berlin Wall. When it happened, I was more upset that coverage of the historic event was overriding a new *Simpsons* episode.

The Angry Brit pushed on. "You idiots don't know anything about Germany except for Hitler and Oktoberfest."

I thought this was a bad time to lay on him my vast knowledge of *Hogan's Heroes* trivia that I have in my head, but trust me, I was ready to Col. Klink his ass.

"I bet you don't even know where Berlin even is!" he slurred.

My gut instinct was to quickly answer "Germany", but at least I was smart enough to know that's not what he meant.

He moved in closer and traced his finger in an outline on my chest. "This is Germany," he said as he repeatedly traced. "Tell me where Berlin is?"

At this point the open bar no longer seemed as appealing. I just wanted to get my drink on for free and maybe talk to a pretty girl. Instead, some drunk with bad teeth and horrid breath was finger-diddling my solar plexus and asking me high school geography questions. And worst of all? I didn't know the answer to the simple geography question. Even if I didn't recall that from Mr. Vallincourt's class seven years prior, I should have picked it up during the endless newscasts that had been unavoidable since the Wall came down. *And yet I HAD avoided them.*

His Tanqueray-scented breath washed over me as he demanded an answer. I took a guess and pointed to the middle of the imaginary map of Germany he'd imprinted on my chest. He smiled. *Had I guessed right?* Then I realized it wasn't a smile, it was a dreadful British leer. Droplets of spittle flew through the air as he yelled, "Stupid!! Just like all the rest! It's up here. Right here!" as he poked me over my meager right pectoral where his Berlin on my make-believe chest map was. "It's right here. Here! HERE!!! How can all of you Americans be so effing stupid? How can you get any dinner if you don't eat your figgy pudding!!" I may have made up that last bit, but only because when he yelled he sounded just like the guy in that Pink Floyd song. His quick-rising ire would have been extremely funny, but I couldn't see the humor because I was pretty sure he was going to tear through my rib cartilage with his boney British digit as he repeatedly attacked my "chest Berlin" over and over again. Just when I didn't think I could take anymore, he stopped, took a final swig of the drink in his hand, calmly placed it on the table and walked away. That spot on my chest was black and blue for close to a week.

The next morning at work, I flinched when I first saw him walking down the hall at me. He was clear-headed, smiling and walked with the élan of one of Fagin's merry pickpockets. As we passed in the hall, he nodded his head slightly in greeting, as he usually did, and moved on. He still had no idea who I was. If they fingerprinted my sternum, I could have proved the attack had taken place, but I never brought it up again. Mostly because I didn't want to take any more pop geography quizzes.

Even though the place had more than its share of kooks, there was one nice woman who stood out for an entirely different reason, the lovely Lottie Mae. She was this unbelievably charming woman who worked in the promotions department. She was an attractive middle-aged brunette who was strikingly statuesque. I'm six-foot-three and in heels she was even taller than me. She was probably close to two decades older than me at the time, but she was quite the beauty. And just as importantly, she was the sweetest woman you could ever meet. Even in my early days, when almost no one spoke to me, she went out of her way to be kind and gentle and offer an encouraging word.

At some point early in my tenure someone mentioned, as happened to every man who ever worked in that building, that she once appeared in the magazine. It was true, she'd once been a Pet of the Month and had eventually gotten a job at the organization and moved up through the ranks. Now imagine if you found out that a sweet, middle-aged woman you worked with once posed for nude pictures, wouldn't you want to see them? And with the entire catalog of *Penthouse* back issues stored at my desk, it was literally about ninety seconds from the time I found out she'd once posed to the time when I was actually holding the issue in my hands, thumbing through it greedily.

I found the pictorial right away, and immediately felt ashamed. This woman was so nice, and now I was looking at her in her birthday suit. She was just as lovely as a young woman and her statuesque physique certainly filled the pages, but I quickly closed the magazine and never really looked at it again. It seemed like such an invasion of the privacy of someone I knew. I met plenty of the girls who'd posed for the magazine over the years, but none made me feel as odd as I did looking at Lottie Mae. Maybe it was her sweet disposition or her maternal nature, but something about looking at those pics felt like crossing the line. In her defense, she never shied away from her modeling past and was proud of her earlier work. And continued to be a doll to work with the whole time I knew her.

18
THE START OF MY TRANSFORMATION

My early experiences, surviving almost getting fired and practically bankrupting the company gave me a new level of confidence. I was no longer a newbie; I was a grizzled veteran who had survived a trial by fire. At the tender age of twenty-three, I was doing pretty well.

New York was still evolving at the time. It had come out of its miserable cash-strapped '70s, seen the economic success of the '80s and then the downfall of the markets on Black Friday in 1988. But somehow, the hallowed halls of *Penthouse* still had the surreal feel of the late 1960s. Male superiors called female underlings "babe" and "sweetie" and "toots." With all of that overt sexism and the milieu of naked lady pictures we all worked in, *Penthouse* was still ahead of the curve in putting women in positions of power. Bob Guccione was the owner, but his partner (who would later become his wife) was the president of the company. And there were at least as many female managers as there were men. So there was an odd mix of sexism and women's lib going on in the Gooch's kingdom.

My department was firmly entrenched in that 1960's era *Mad Men* landscape. Managers still had secretaries who prepared their coffee, answered their phones and brought them their lunch. Hell, they even took dictation. This seemed totally normal to me, because I didn't really know anything else. So I started acting exactly like the rest of the men in my department, calling the secretaries "babe" and "toots." Coming from the skinny, clueless kid that I was, I'm sure it sounded ridiculous. Especially when the women I was talking to were all at least a decade older than I. What an ass. But somehow I thought it worked.

Oddly, emulating these anachronistic behaviors of my superiors had a transformative effect on me over time. Playing the role of confidently cocky business guy actually resulted in me *becoming* a more confidently cocky business guy. I didn't notice it, but I was slowly developing into the self-assured, poised guy that I would become later in life.

19
My First Pet of the Year Party

Every issue of *Penthouse* had a Pet of the Month. It was our version of Hef's Playmate of the Month. And of course, once a year a big hoopla would surround a special Pet of the Year issue. It was made-up spectacle, but spectacle nonetheless. Whoever was chosen for this role was given, I think, a car, a cash bonus and special duties as *Penthouse* ambassador. But all I remember was the buzz around the office leading up to my first Pet of the Year Party. The winner was announced at a big blowout party that was really held as an excuse to wine and dine the advertising community to entice them to spend their money on our pages. Around the office, being invited to this party was seen as quite a perk.

As a low-level member of the production team, I probably should not have been included, but one of the amiable secretaries got me on the list and I was formally invited. I remember getting the fancy invitation. It was a very formal invite printed on hard card stock with, of course, a barely clad young woman in red lingerie and a come-hither stare on the front. The party was at the Puck Building in downtown Manhattan, a historic old building just north of Manhattan's Little Italy. I wasn't sure what to expect. I'd heard stories from everyone about these parties in the past and they all seemed legendary. Celebrities galore, the best food and booze, true decadence. I was geared up for the night of my life. What I ended up at felt more like a really nice wedding.

The place was decked out with lots of gauzy white drapes hanging everywhere. There were different bars and cocktail areas set up and hundreds of people milling about as I wandered from room to room. I saw a lot of the same thing: guys in suits, scarfing down free drinks and looking for hot chicks. I saw a grand total of two celebrities. The first was the famous artist Leroy Neiman. He was instantly recognizable, with that telltale handlebar mustache. Second was Gilbert Gottfried. He was a tiny wisp of a man who looked extremely uncomfortable every time people came up to introduce themselves and say they were big fans. And that was it. In truth, it was actually pretty boring. Probably because I didn't have any friends to hang out with. But the guys who were there schmoozing clients seemed to be having a blast and everyone was getting pretty well oiled. Eventually, an odd hush fell over the crowd. I tried to figure out what had happened. There was a rising murmur coming from the opposite corner of the room. I made my way over, as did everybody else. Then I saw what was causing such a stir. The man himself had arrived.

Bob Guccione made his grand entrance with a bevy of beautiful *Penthouse* Pets and the energy of the room was instantly changed. All the sales guys brought their clients over to take pictures with the Pets and the music really started pumping. That's when I made my move. My move to leave, that is. The party was on a Tuesday night and I still had a ninety-minute commute home and then back to work in the morning, so with midnight fast approaching, it was time for me to get my Cinderella ass out of there.

When I staggered in to work exhausted the next morning, there was another buzz in the office. Not the buzz of excitement from the previous day when everyone was stoked about the party. This had a different feel. When I asked around, someone showed me that morning's *New York Post*. On the cover was a picture of the Pet of the Year party invite, under the screaming headline, "Invitation to Death!" Sadly, it seems that a young man in the advertising community had attended the party, maybe had a little too much to drink, then took a wrong turn walking back to his subway entrance. He was mugged, stabbed and left to die. It was a tragic event, but I'm sure if it had just been a guy coming home from a night in the bar with the boys, it would have been a two-paragraph story buried on page eleven, but since *Penthouse* was involved, they made it into a huge story. Another tragic, cautionary New York tale.

20
THE RETURN OF THE RCE
(RESIDENT COMPUTER EXPERT)

I didn't know much about computers, but I was starting to get the hang of them. I knew how to do my reports and spreadsheets, and in time had all of our financial stuff on my behemoth of a desktop computer, an IBM clone running an early version of Windows. One morning I strolled into work and the Resident Computer Expert, who'd seen through the sham that I was in my original interview, was sitting in front of my computer. I don't think I'd seen him outside of his dark, subterranean lair of an office in all my time there, so I was certainly surprised to see his hulking, unkempt girth plopped on my seat.

"Good morning, what's going on?" I tried to say. Before I could even finish, he was sputtering at me through an ash-choked cigarette, "When was the last time you backed up this machine?!!"

"Huh?" I responded in a confused tone that only seemed to anger the beast.

"THE BACK-UP. WHEN WAS THE LAST TIME YOU DID A BACKUP?!!"

I really had no idea what he was talking about. I thought he was going to charge at me, if only he could un-wedge himself from my chair.

Someone from his department poked his head over the cubicle wall to help out. "He wants to know the last time you backed up your hard drive onto the floppies?"

I still had no clue what anyone was talking about and RCE was getting madder and madder. "TELL ME YOU'VE BEEN BACKING UP YOUR COMPUTER!!" he screamed in a murderous rage.

"How do I do that?" I asked innocently enough, but it was too much for him to handle. He slammed his hand on the desk, his full ashtray exploded all over the place and he stormed off in the direction of Howard's office.

I turned to the guy over the cubicle. "What the hell just happened?"

The guy explained that RCE was installing some new software on everyone's machines and had been in my cubicle for quite a while before I arrived. He also explained what "backing up" was. Once a week we were supposed to hook up this device to our computers that saved all of our data to a separate drive; that way if anything happened to the machine, we'd always have access to our data. It made perfect sense to me and I gladly would have done it. *If someone had told me to!*

But for now, I was left sitting in a seat that was still uncomfortably warm from RCE's butt, staring at a dead computer screen and a keyboard covered in cigarette ashes. Before long, they exited Howard's office. RCE stomped back to his lair as Howard came over to see me.

I had flashbacks to my near-firing after the paper incident

a while back, and I thought I was once again in big trouble. Howard asked what had happened and I said I didn't really know. He asked why I hadn't backed up my computer. I had to think quickly. I couldn't feign ignorance because I'd gotten my job based on made up computer experience. I quickly made up a lie. "At my old job, our backups were automatically done by the servers," I stammered. I didn't know if that even made sense, but neither did Howard. He knew less about computers than I ever did. He had a bright, shiny one sitting on his desk that was used mostly as a paperweight. Luckily, he took my answer at face value and walked away. I heard him go into RCE's office and close the door.

A few minutes later they both came into my cubicle. RCE was much calmer now and just sat down in front of my machine and started clacking away. Howard explained that RCE had been upgrading something or other on my machine. I assume he explained it wrong, not because I understood anything, but because the way RCE was snorting crankily in the background. The end result was that I lost everything that was on my computer. This didn't really strike me at first as anything terrible; I was just relieved that I wasn't in trouble. In fact, it was RCE who was in deeper shit for mucking around on my machine. When he was done working on my computer, everything seemed to be back to normal. He gave me a gruff walkthrough of how to back up my data in the future and barked at me to make sure I did it at least once a week, without fail.

Finally, peace was restored in my cubicle and I could start my day. It didn't take me long to realize just how screwed I really was. My computer was now completely blank. All of the spreadsheets and files I'd put together since I'd started were no longer there.

Gone, baby, gone. So that's what he meant when he said I lost everything. I was devastated.

I went to Howard's office flummoxed. "So what does this mean? Can he get my files back?!"

"Nope. He said they were gone forever. I guess you'll just have to re-create them."

Since Howard didn't know how the damn computer even worked, he didn't quite comprehend the amount of work that would entail.

"Me? Why should I have to do it? He's the one who screwed up my computer."

He let out a huge sigh. I could tell he'd already spent way too much time discussing a problem that he could barely understand to begin with.

"Well, you really should have been backing up your machine..."

And he let that linger just long enough, so that I took it to mean, it could really be my fault and he was going to call me out on my earlier defense. I didn't feel like I had any options, so I retreated to my desk. As I left, Howard mentioned that he had a meeting downtown in the afternoon, but he should be back by five. *Fore!*

Back in my finally cooled seat, I began the painstaking task of re-creating every spreadsheet, file and report I had completed to date. It took me months to get back on track.

I was pissed at RCE and pissed at the company for letting a guy screw me like that without any ramifications. And then I thought back to my own paper-purchasing debacle. My own failures had placed the company in dire financial peril. His mess-up cost a junior-level employee a few extra weeks of work. Neither was punished. *What kind of company was this?*

21
Me, Interview Somebody?

One day Howard came over and announced that we'd be getting a secretary for our department. I was a little confused. I didn't need a secretary and I didn't really know what Howard did, but I couldn't imagine he needed a secretary to help him do it. I didn't really understand how the place worked at the time, but I would later learn that there was money in the budget for a secretary for the department so if they didn't hire one, we'd just lose that money. No one ever wants to lose money from their budget. That's how I, a company tenderfoot in a job I wasn't qualified for, found myself interviewing a string of middle-aged women who couldn't figure out why their future employment was in the hands of a hungover young man who could be their son.

Howard would have the final say on whom we hired, but he wanted them to chat with me first to determine if they were qualified. Ironically, if anyone knew about being *un*qualified, it was me! I think the real reason they made me the first interview was that I had to ask them if they were okay working with the salacious material contained within our pages. That's why I spent the afternoon showing pictures of naked young ladies to modest middle-aged women. Looking back, I'm sure there must have been something vaguely illegal, probably immoral and definitely unseemly about making women look at pictures of other naked women to make sure they could do so without flinching before having a shot at the job. But the fact that they were in the *Penthouse* Building, and sat beneath pictures of our lurid covers in the lobby while waiting for the interview should have weeded out the demure and weak-of-heart candidates.

Eventually, we hired a fifty-something woman. Not surprisingly, Howard wasn't there on her first day, so he asked me to show her the ropes. Not really knowing what "the ropes" were, I just showed her what I did. We went through the paper orders, my budget reports, my spreadsheets, etc. By day's end, I was feeling like quite the professional…imparting my wisdom to an underling.

The next morning I was quite surprised to get called into Howard's office as soon as I walked in. He was in there with an HR rep. *What the hell had I done now?* And that was exactly what they asked me. "What the hell did you do now?" I didn't know what they were talking about until they explained further. It seems the new secretary had already quit! My first underling! And she didn't even last twenty-four hours!!

They figured I must have done something to scare her off. And they were right, I had scared her off. But not with inappropriate behavior or our explicit subject matter. She was a true old-school secretary who'd spent most of her career answering phones, taking dictation and fetching coffee. My "professionalism" showing her spreadsheets and budget reports scared her into feeling extremely under-qualified for the job. I sat there, once again, thinking I was going to be in trouble. But after they conferred for a bit, they realized it was better that someone like that who didn't want to grow in the role and learn the business of the department was better to be rid of.

Ironically, her skill set, or lack thereof, was really no different than mine when I was hired. But where I figured I could make it up as I went along, she decided to run from it.

We ended up finding a suitable replacement a week later who was younger and not afraid to learn more than just answering phones, etc. The only problem was that she needed a little more money to leave her old job. Howard agreed to it and she was hired. Now I had a big problem. The $24,000 they offered her was the same amount I was making. *Son of a bitch!*

I was so aggravated. I was barely scraping by from paycheck to paycheck. I know it took big balls for me to be upset at whatever salary I was making, especially since, A) I was wholly unqualified for the job I was doing, and B) constantly getting in trouble, getting called on the carpet and seemingly always minutes away from being fired. But I was upset. I thought I'd made some big improvements over time and was doing a semi-decent job at that point. Now I was going to be making the same amount of money as the person answering our phones and doing our filing? I sat and stewed for a bit.

By the end of the day I was in quite the foul mood. I wasn't sure if I should raise a stink or just keep my mouth shut. If I forced the issue, was there a chance they would fire me? I wasn't sure if I wanted to make that gamble. If I lost this gig, rent wasn't going to get paid and I'd be in a whole lot of trouble. I finally decided I had to say something. I went in there, with a fully thought-out list of reasons about why I didn't think it was fair that they were going to pay the secretary the same as me. I was ready to detail how far I'd come since I'd started. How I'd updated the whole department, refined our reporting process and cleaned up my paper debacle. I had a whole list of accomplishments—I was ready for a fight.

I went in to Howard's office, closed the door and told him I was upset. "What's the matter?" He said with the calm, cool demeanor of a man counting down the hours to his 5:30 train back to Darien, Connecticut. (It must've been raining that day, cancelling his afternoon "meeting.")

"It's the new secretary," I began. "I can't believe you're paying her the same as me!"

"What? No, we're only paying her twenty-four," he explained.

"That's what I make!" I squealed in a voice more fitting to someone ten years my junior. And female.

Howard stared silently at me, trying to put all the pieces together in his head.

Finally he asked, "You're at twenty-four a year?"

"Yes!" I said with still a bit too much squeak.

"Be right back," he said as he hopped off his seat and headed out the door.

I sat there in the silence, much like I'd done that very first day when I thought I was going to be bounced out of the interview for lying about my computer experience. Now I was sitting in the same chair, waiting for…I didn't know what. I started replaying our conversation in my head. Wait a minute. *Did he just ask me how much I was making? Did he really not know? What the hell?*

I didn't have to wait too long. He came back pretty quickly. He had a big grin on his face as he explained that the Cheeky Brit had approved a three-thousand-dollar raise for me. "Satisfied?" he asked.

I matched his smile with an even wider one. I thanked him and rushed out of his office.

On the way back to Grand Central, I started reviewing the recent path life had led me down. I'd truly wandered down the rabbit hole that was *Penthouse Inc.* I'd gotten a job I wasn't qualified for, done numerous things that could have or should have gotten me fired, and thrown my first corporate hissy fit. Not only had I never been booted out on my ass, but I had just gotten a decent raise out of it. I still really didn't know what the hell was going on, but it was hard not to believe that I could succeed in this world. The worst part is that at that young age, I thought this was how the whole world worked. That this was a traditional corporate environment. And I was succeeding. You do not have to skip to the end to realize that it does not end well. But for the time being, I thought that I could ride the wave forever.

22
HOLY OVERTIME, BATMAN!

In addition to ordering all of the paper for the magazines, the other big part of my job was analyzing production costs. Which meant I would look at the budget we had for each issue, compare it to how much we actually spent printing it and write up a report detailing the variances. It was as deadly boring as it sounds. Most of the magazines weren't too challenging, but *Penthouse* was the tough one. It continuously ran over budget, issue after issue. The main reason was almost always the same, printing delays. As I mentioned earlier our magazines were printed mostly in Des Moines, Iowa. The huge printing plant's massive machines ran 24/7 producing not just our books, but hundreds of other titles. Somewhere in their calendar our print run was scheduled to occur. If we were late getting them our materials, it would cause a slow-down in the process that would delay the presses and hold up the rest of their business. That's why they built in penalties to all contracts for any delays. And that's what we were paying. Every single month. We're talking tens of thousands of dollars.

I really was trying to be better at my job. The first few months I would just copy Jack's explanations from the prior month's report and attribute X amount of dollars to the press holding fee. The more I started understanding the process, the more I tried to get to the bottom of all the late fees. I figured if I could root out the real problem, maybe I could streamline the process, save the company a ton of money and look like a hero.

The deeper I dug, the more I uncovered about the craziness of this privately held company. It turned out that all of our lateness problems had to do with our pictorials. Granted, we occasionally had special one-shot photo essays that were timely in nature and were worked on up until the very last minute, such as the Madonna nudes that we published in 1985, or the Vanessa Williams spread from 1984 that resulted in her losing her Miss America title. But for the most part our pictorials were just regular photos. Plain old naked Pet of the Month pics that looked exactly like every other naked girl we'd had in the book before. In a normal world, these should have been the least timely things in the magazine. Hell, all of the pictures for the year could have been picked and designed on January 1 and been ready to go. But that's not how things worked.

You see, Bob Guccione personally picked out and approved the layouts himself, like he'd done since doing it for the first time at his kitchen table in England for that very first issue. But as much as things had changed over the years, Bob still liked to stay involved. Unfortunately, Bob was an extremely slow worker. It was legend that he would stay up all hours of the night crafting layouts or working on his paintings. Not unusual behavior for a true artist, but kind of a tough schedule when an entire empire bows to your commands. So long before I came along, it became accepted practice that schedules would be set, and Bob would ignore them and approve materials on his own timeframe, usually a day or two late, which ended up costing the magazine tons of money in overtime charges. When the company was wildly successful and money was pouring in from every direction, I'm sure this was just seen as an odd quirk by a guy who could afford it. But by the time I got there, the coffers were not as full as they'd been and wasting money like this was not in anyone's best interest.

It seemed unfathomable to me that someone wouldn't just explain the truth to Bob. He was pissing away money by not having the magazine done on time. Again, this wasn't urgent stuff that needed to be done at the last minute. It was pictures of naked girls that sat on his desk until he eventually got around to signing off on them. This was another sign that something was not right in this company. It was the first true glimpse I had of the Emperor's New Clothes policy that the place ran on. Nobody wanted to piss off the boss, so they shuffled everything under the rug. I would write in my reports that we were $20,000 over budget for this or that month and by blaming it on overtime charges, everyone knew what I meant.

As money and budgets got tighter, they started playing with the schedules behind Bob's back. They would tell him things were due a week before they actually were. That would work briefly and then we'd fall behind schedule again, so they'd bump his schedule two weeks ahead of the real thing, then three. It was crazy, but everyone would rather find other places to cut money than tell Bob to turn his shit in on time. And all the while, our printers gladly collected a fortune in overtime fees.

23
MOVING INTO NYC

Whilst plugging away at my job and actually starting to get pretty good at it, I still knew that this wasn't what I wanted to do with the rest of my life. It was a nagging feeling in the back of my head that sometimes crept to the forefront, but I would usually just drown it in beer and move on. A year after the incident with the new secretary that got me a raise, I was up for another salary review. Howard explained how happy they were with my work and laughed off the miserable start I'd had. He gave me another three-thousand-dollar raise, bumping me up to $30,000/year. Again, it seemed great. Not that long ago, I'd been bussing tables for $4.60/hour, and now I was pulling down a decent salary.

This was the time to make my move. I'd grown tired of living in Connecticut. The endless commute to and from the city, made much worse by the fact that I would constantly stay in after work and revel with whoever had an expense account and taking the drunk train home after midnight only to have to fall out of bed at six the next morning for the return trip. I was still living paycheck to paycheck, but with this new raise I decided to make the big jump to move in to Manhattan.

Of course, in keeping with the ongoing theme, I once again drastically underestimated my financial needs. A train pass from Connecticut was costing me $150/month. My new raise added another $160/month. So when I found a place to split with a buddy for only $300 more a month, I thought I would be able to make the move seamlessly. I was wrong. Again. I did not take into account the added expense of everything in Manhattan. Plus, with living just a ten-minute subway ride from the office, I spent a lot more nights out carousing. I was making more money that I'd ever seen in my life and I was still just scraping by. Of course a wise man would just cut back on the nights out and try to sock some money away. But I was not a wise man. I was an idiot with a job at *Penthouse*. So I lived on cereal and Ramen noodles, and persevered.

24
MOVIN' ON UP

As I entered my third year at *Penthouse*, I was doing my job about as well as it could be done. I'd resolved my earlier paper crisis and kept a good handle on that side of the biz. I was getting to know the printing side better and better. And the reports I was writing were actually pretty professional. The fact that Jack's were handwritten not that long ago made it easier for mine to look better just by virtue of being done on a computer. And month after month, I found new and creative ways to describe our endless overtime expenses. I still didn't really like my job, but I started to think that maybe that's just how grown-up life really is. You get a job. You trudge on trying to make the most of it, and then you go home. If you're lucky, in forty or so years you retire and they give you a cheap gold watch.

At some point, instead of sending the reports up to finance I would hand-deliver them and I started buddying up with Tim, the senior financial analyst. He was a pretty normal guy, and we liked a lot of the same things (beer, sports, chicken wings—the basis for all of my friendships for the first thirty years of my life.

And come to think of it, every one since.). We'd sit in his tiny office and commiserate about our jobs for a bit. And when I say tiny, I mean *tiny*. It was basically a closet, with cubicle furniture wedged in. The room actually had less actual square footage than the cubicles that lined the rest of the department, but it was an office. When you're stuck in cubicle hell, the dream is to someday have a door. A door at least gives you the occasional semblance of privacy. Since his place was so small, he just had the office chair that he sat in (that faced his behemoth of a computer) and another small chair wedged in next to it. Because of the room restraints, both chairs faced the same way, so we'd sit and shoot the shit, sitting side by side, like two guys riding a bus.

Other than Tim, I really didn't know anyone else in the finance department until I had to join Tim's boss, Pete, and a few other finance guys on a trip to our printing plant. It was some type of audit trip, and since every roll of paper had to be counted and verified again (after my earlier paper debacle) they brought me to do all of the dirty work, crawling through the mountains of dreck-covered walls of paper.

The trip was just another free journey for me. A chance to eat and drink on the company dime. I was still a clueless kid with no money, so I always took full advantage. I'm sure I did absolutely nothing on that trip that would make Pete think I would make a good finance employee. But as I would encounter endless times in the future of my career, my personality got me a lot further than my brains.

A few months later, Kathy Keeton fired the company's budget director. Spectacularly. One of those fired-on-the spot moments that seemed to happen a lot on the third floor and had the company buzzing for days. I didn't know the guy, so other than idle office chatter that got me out of doing work for a bit, it really didn't affect me. Or so I thought.

The following week they promoted my buddy Tim to the budget director position. Then he and Pete called me up to the third floor. They wanted to offer me Tim's job as senior financial analyst. *Huh?* I hadn't even been a junior financial analyst. *Was this a joke?* Apparently not. Tim vouched for my skills in producing the budget reports for my department, and Pete remembered me as a smart, good guy from that earlier trip. These two accountants in business suits sat and stared at a dopey twenty-four-year-old in wrinkled khakis and a stained shirt and waited for an answer. I hemmed and hawed and asked how much it paid. Pete said "Thirty-four thousand." That was all I needed to hear. It was four grand more than I was making, so for the second time in this building, I accepted a job whose responsibilities I didn't even understand and certainly wasn't qualified for.

I walked out of his office thinking about the money and feeling pretty good. As I made my way past the cubicles full of dour, polyester-suit-wearing accountants, I started doubting my decision. *Was this my new life? What was I doing working for the finance department?* I had finally gotten my college degree in psychology. And after those earlier writing courses, I now had creative aspirations rattling around somewhere in the back of my brain. Had I just signed up for a lifetime of number-crunching?

As I started trying to figure out what I'd just committed to, I passed by Tim's office and the light bulb went on over my head! I rushed back to Pete's office.

"This new job means I get Tim's old office, right?" They simply nodded their heads yes and that was all I needed to hear. *I now had a door. A door! A glorious door!*

25
MY LIFE AS A
FINANCIAL ANALYST

My fears of being turned into an accountant were extremely overrated. When I started in my new role as senior financial analyst, I was actually much better suited for it than I thought. It was a lot of the same stuff I'd been doing downstairs, except instead of comparing actual spending versus budget for just the manufacturing department, I was doing it for the whole company. It was a lot of OCD attention to detail that I'd found I was pretty good at. The hardest part was writing up the variance explanations, which were difficult at first because I didn't know how the other departments ran or what they did. But I slowly figured that out, too.

When I was in Production, folks just kind of ignored me. But now that I was part of Finance and actually had a hand in their budgets and spending, they treated me with a little more respect. It was undeserved, but it still felt good. Getting answers I needed from folks was a lot easier than when I was a clueless rube downstairs.

The most important thing about my job, as Tim drilled into me incessantly from the start, was that I was now privy to certain financial information that was NOT for the general population. The most important of these was everyone's salaries. What people make was always a huge topic for discussion and gossip, as I'm sure it is in every office. But it was especially true at a place as wacky as *Penthouse*, where there was such a cross-section of old-time loyalists, hotshot hired guns, lifers, etc. Since most of the jobs I've held since then have always involved me being privy to what every one around me makes, it is hard to remember back to a time when that was such a huge thing to be concerned about. And since the only other person's salary I knew in the company was my earlier beef about our secretary making as much as me, I was very curious.

Curiosity quickly led to disgust and dismay. I learned something that would become apparent for the rest of my corporate career. Those who do the most work don't necessarily make the most money. Sure, some of the well-compensated folks were valuable and worth every penny, but there was a lot of bloat on that payroll. Worse than finding out what everyone earned was the fact that everyone in the building now realized that I knew what everyone earned. People who had barely acknowledged my existence suddenly became very chummy with the hopes that I would spill some of my newfound secrets. But I was good; I held firm. I did what was right for the company and also for them. Knowing what the people around you make only leads to anger and resentment. There's always going to be somebody making more than you who you don't think is worth it, and that knowledge can drive you batshit-crazy.

As I learned more and more about the company's fiscal health, I found that the bloat wasn't just relegated to the payroll. There was excessive waste *everywhere*. The more time I spent learning the financial workings of the company, the more I was astounded that the place was still in business.

Expense-report spending was totally out of control. Of course, I should have known this, based on all the times I went out with work people and someone dropped the whole tab on their credit card, but I didn't expect the numbers to be so huge. Then there were the various ventures that had failed over the years, but were still on the books. An unsuccessful clothing line, abandoned television projects, various video start-ups. The one that stood out to me the most was Bob's Atlantic City project. He had originally dreamed of opening a *Penthouse* casino there since the town had welcomed gambling back in 1976. He began construction in the late '70s but never got past the steel girder stage. From then on it was mired in endless legal wrangling that was still running up incredible lawyer bills in the early nineties. Bob had never been successful acquiring a gambling license (something he believed was due to wrongly conceived mob ties stemming from his Italian heritage). I never understood what the lawyers were billing us for and how it could rack up so many expenses over the years, but I'm sure the lawyers came to see the situation as a bottomless pit of billable hours, so they just kept at it.

In addition to the big wastes of money I constantly saw, I was also surprised at some of the little things that crossed my desk. I once saw an expense report for Pete, the head of my department, and he was writing off a bag of cough drops. *Really? The CFO of an international company and you can't spring the three bucks for a bag of Halls out of your own pocket?*

One of the most bizarre items I saw was a monthly storage bill. A storage bill wasn't that far out of the ordinary. We paid to store paper inventory, magazine issues, any number of things really. But this one was different. It seems we were paying a company to store the frozen semen of Bob and Kathy's two dogs. Yes, their Rhodesian Ridgebacks were magnificent animals, but were they so spectacular that their fluids needed to be locked away in a freezer somewhere? What was the game plan? If one of the dogs happened to pass, were they going to use the puppy juice to inseminate another dog and make a replacement? Or did Bob have plans to begin a doggy cloning company that would then create him an army of his precious pooches? This wasn't as absurd a theory as you would think based on his earlier nuclear energy investments and later conversations I would have with the man himself. I was so puzzled by this bizarre expense that I asked a few of the accountants about it and they just shrugged their shoulders. It was nothing new to them.

I still wonder where that frozen dog sperm ended up.

I doubt it was the same company, but I like to think it was in a freezer at the place where Walt Disney and Ted Williams had their heads cryogenically frozen. That would be just my luck if I were to go the severed-and-frozen noggin route after my passing. *Let's see, I'm going to be frozen here for quite a while, I wonder who they're going to put me next to? I hope it's Walt or the Splendid Splinter. Nope, it's just a bucket of dog jizz from the Upper East Side. Wonderful.*

26
IT'S GAME TIME

After a few months of learning my new budgeting job and faring fairly well, Tim decided it was time for me to start getting involved with the budget presentations to Kathy. Originally, I thought it was because he trusted me and wanted me to succeed. I eventually realized that he wanted to groom me to take over these duties so that he wouldn't have to do them anymore. Spending time with the big boss lady wasn't really seen as a perk of ascending through the ranks, it just meant more time in front of an unstable individual who could fire you at any moment.

Tim prepped me for my first big meeting with Kathy. She wanted to review how her two magazines were doing. She was president of the entire company, but her two babies were *Omni*, the decade-old science fiction/fact magazine and *Longevity*, a new publication that she'd launched about the art and science of staying young. She was extremely proud of both titles and saw them as the preeminent magazines in their fields. What they were, in reality, were huge profit-suckers. *Omni* was a lavishly produced, gorgeous-to-look-at-book that cost way more to produce than it ever made. It had never turned a profit. And *Longevity* was another wildly expensive book without a true audience or advertising base. To her credit, *Longevity* may have been a bit ahead of its time. Done right and marketed to the right crowd a decade later, when folks were more concerned about aging, natural health and the environment, I think a well-done *Longevity* could have been a modest success. But in 1991, she wasn't going for a modest success: she was shooting for the moon. And burning through payloads of cash in the process.

So our job was to massage the numbers. Tim and I prepared to review a very generic overview of the most favorable numbers we could put together for her. When the day came, I was more than ready. I knew my facts inside and out, but Tim had told me over and over again, to not dive too deep into the details or specifics. This was for two reasons. The first was that the deeper you dove, the harder it was to mask the truth. The second was that Kathy didn't really understand the numbers. She, like her husband, preferred to deal with things on a "big-picture" level. The details did not interest them, so they did not even try to comprehend them.

At the last minute our 11 AM meeting was pushed back to 12:30 and turned into a lunch meeting. I didn't really care, but it seemed to make Tim apprehensive, so that trickled down to me. When the appointed time came, Tim and I made our way to her office. Unlike the drab, grey dinginess of the rest of our finance world, her office was ornate, with a fine wood desk, lush white rug and artwork everywhere representing her South African homeland. I even think I remember a pair of tusks, but I can't be sure. It was all a bit of a blur because as we walked in, Kathy was finishing up another meeting. As she welcomed us in, she complained how hot it was and removed her jacket. This should not have been a problem, but it was quite apparent that the sheer silk halter-top she had on really was meant to be worn *under something*. Her saline-swollen breasts were barely covered. This was not a good way to start the biggest meeting to date of my career.

I'm sure at this point some of you are writing me off as some immature horndog acting inappropriately, but it was just too bizarre. It's not even like she was doing it as a power trip, daring me to look or anything like that. She just thought it was totally fine to have an important finance meeting while sitting in a thousand-dollar chair with her titties hanging out. And it got worse. She wasn't sitting behind her desk, she was over by a couch and chairs setup. Tim quickly, and knowingly, grabbed the other chair, so I had no place to sit but on the couch. It was a lovely couch. Probably worth as much as I made in three months of work. But it was all form over function. It looked nice, but I knew I was in trouble as soon as I sat down. It was a very low couch with thick pillowy cushions that enveloped me. At six foot three, I usually have trouble sitting on most couches. My long legs end up at weird angles and I perpetually look like a newborn colt trying to stand. This couch was even worse. My ass sank to the floor and my knees were just about at chin level. I tried to balance my finance binders and notepad as best I could, but I looked ridiculous. I know that I looked ridiculous, because Tim, who was usually nothing but the most reserved professional in Kathy's presence, was having trouble keeping a straight face.

We dove right in, with Kathy raising a couple of immediate and pressing concerns she had about *Longevity*. They were not questions I expected, and certainly not questions that were important in the slightest way for the financial health of her magazine. Tim handled the questions deftly and put her at ease like the experienced "yes man" he was. Throughout their lengthy exchange, I realized that she had yet to even acknowledge my presence. We'd walked in. Tim and I had sat down. She started talking to Tim and I was just some awkwardly folded human pretzel sitting two feet away from her. Worst of all, since I was sitting at an angle from her, as she talked and talked, waving at the air emphatically, I had an unobstructed view of her entire right breast. Again, this was not erotic or sexy in any way. It was just there. And I knew I shouldn't look at it, but like a car accident, I couldn't look away.

At some point, Tim finally forced her to acknowledge my presence by saying, "Good question, I think Steve here has those numbers." He was probably also trying to wake me out of my bosom-induced stupor. I snapped back to reality and fumbled through my binder. Tim kindly repeated the question so I knew what the hell I was looking for. When I gave her the answer, she finally looked at me for the first time and smiled. "Oh, that's wonderful. Very good indeed." I forget the specifics, but I'm sure we told her something insignificant that made it sound like the book was doing better than expected. The spin was the most important part of these meetings. Tim, the budget director, was the latest in a long line of budget directors. Most of them had been fired because they hadn't spun the numbers correctly, hadn't been able to cover their own asses or possibly (as I currently feared) had been caught staring at her naughty bits for too long.

But my answer seemed to satisfy her and we moved on to other matters. Before long the door opened and the "lunch" part of the meeting began. I'd been in lunch meetings before and it usually just meant pizza in the conference room or bringing your deli sandwich into somebody else's office. This was different. This consisted of china, crystal and fancy silverware. WTF? Tim glanced at me and quietly mouthed, "Just do what I do." A fancy, four-star-restaurant-quality lunch was placed in front of me on the coffee table. Tim and Kathy both started eating while discussing various issues. Trapped on the couch like I was, there was nowhere for me to go. The only way I could wedge myself closer to the edge of the couch so I could reach my plate was to sit with my legs akimbo, like a giraffe bending down to nibble at a branch on the ground. With each movement, I feared knocking into the glass-top table, currently covered in expensive china and crystal. I don't remember exactly what the meal was, but I know it had a sauce. A sauce I was desperately afraid of. I did not know if it was physically possible to get a bite of anything on that plate to my mouth without some of it dripping on to the expensive white couch or the probably much more expensive white rug. I tried my best, but ended up just pushing food around my plate like a stubborn toddler. Luckily, I was still mostly invisible to Kathy.

Finally, the plates were cleared. Tim lobbed a few more of the easier questions at me and that was it. We were done. We weren't done because we had covered everything; we were done because Kathy's next meeting was there. We had, in fact covered nothing of substance with regards to the finances of the two magazines. We should have spent the time explaining to her that her two pet projects were bleeding money at a prodigious rate and that drastic moves would need to be made before the whole company went under. But we did not. We chatted about promotional campaigns, over-expectant advertising projections and the importance of pro- ducing a high quality product at any cost. I walked out of my big lunch meeting both confused about the health of the company and starving. I walked to McDonalds for a burger trying to figure out how this place had lasted this long.

27
HOW HAD THEY LASTED THIS LONG?

Bob had quite smartly come up with a formula for a magazine at exactly the right time in American society. *Playboy* had owned the sixties, but *Penthouse*, a raunchier, dirtier book, had gone even further with that formula and made boatloads of money in the process. That huge explosion of cash made anything possible. The investments in Atlantic City, grand Hollywood film productions and a ton of other things were all supported by the cash cow that was *Penthouse Magazine* and the *Penthouse* brand. But a decade later and the mothership was faltering and the various sinkholes were sucking the place dry.

We were all going down with the ship. For some who had been there from the start, it was part of the inevitable rise and fall. For me it was like being lowered on to the Titanic just hours before its infamous collision with the iceberg.

28
SHOWDOWN WITH THE QUEEN

My first big meeting with Kathy had gone well enough. I didn't spill any food, I didn't get caught looking at her chest and, most importantly, I didn't tell her anything she didn't want to hear. My next meeting would not go quite as well. She actually wasn't even supposed to be there. It was a preliminary budget meeting for the following year with all of the department heads. I'd prepared a few basic profit/loss statements for us to review and I wanted to highlight a few areas that needed to be shaped up.

As we were about to begin, Kathy strolled in with one of the editors and joined us. This was nerve-wracking and became even more so when she asked for one of my handouts that everyone was looking over. *This was trouble. These were the REAL numbers!* I'm sure Tim would have able to wiggle his way out of this situation, but I just panicked and gave her the handout. I hoped that if I just sped through things quickly I might be able to get out of this alive. It worked for a while. She looked at my spreadsheet, which had *way* more detail than she was used to, and quickly got bored with it. We went around the table and everyone did what they were accustomed to doing with Kathy, they spoke about how well each of their departments was doing and how great the magazines were. Everyone excelled in the practiced routine of telling the naked empress her new outfit was delightful.

We were almost done and I thought I was going to get out unscathed when I saw Kathy pick up my handout again. "Stephen, something doesn't seem right here, this number must be wrong at the bottom."

The number showed that *Omni Magazine* would lose a great deal of money in the coming year. Just as it had done this current year and every single year before that. I fumbled for an answer. Everyone instantly averted his or her gaze and refused to make eye contact with me. "This can't be right," she reiterated. I tried my best to walk her through the numbers.

Basically, the numbers she usually saw showed revenue for the magazine and a filtered look at expenses, which could make the book look profitable. But in the real world, we had the overhead and so many other expenses that she never saw rightfully charged back that sank the magazine well into the red. I started lamely trying to explain the overhead and other hits to her, but between my nervously shoddy explanations and her inability to understand how the finances worked, she quickly reached her boiling point. With an incredibly screechy voice she yelled at me in front of the entire room. I had obviously done something wrong. I was presenting the wrong numbers. She flew off the handle. I just sat there and took it and she finally just grabbed her stuff and stormed out. There was a long moment of silence before everyone quietly gathered their stuff without saying a word or looking in my direction. The only person to even acknowledge the whole shebang was my old production boss, Howard. He just patted me on the back on his way out and said, "Tough break." I felt like the relief pitcher who had just given up a game-winning grand slam. I hadn't felt like I was about to be fired in quite a while, but those feelings came back very quickly, just like riding a bike.

I sat in my office, once again assuming a security guy would be along at any minute to usher me out of the building. No one came. Eventually I wandered down to Tim's office to see what was going on. I assumed Kathy had left the meeting and gone straight to him or his boss to rave about how incompetent I was. But Tim wasn't there. Neither was Pete. They were out of the office for some other big meeting. I went back to my office and waited. And waited. Nothing happened. Except that the story of my dressing-down had spread throughout the company. People who had no real reason to be in our part of the building were "strolling" by my office to see what was going on. Everyone at the company had heard such stories before and they predicted that I would be fired. I assumed the same thing, which really sucked, because I was still living paycheck to paycheck. *Damn.* At day's end, no one had come to toss me out on my ear, so I simply left.

As I cautiously went to my office the next morning, I could see from the hall that my door was already unlocked and open. Uh-oh. Was one of the security guys boxing up my belongings?

I approached it trembling, to find Tim in there leaving me a note. When he turned to see me, he grumbled and said, "Come with me." I followed him to his office where he closed the door behind us. This was it. He sat behind his desk and stared at me sternly. He could sense the stink of fear in me. I was so bummed I thought I might cry. Then he let out a little smirk. I was confused. Then he started laughing. "What the hell happened in there yesterday?" Wait, why was he laughing? I explained what had gone down, and he just kept laughing and said, "Yeah, that's what I figured." It was the laugh of a guy coming off the front lines, who already knew what it was like to take enemy fire and survive.

Kathy had tracked down Tim's boss, Pete, the day before, but she had cooled a little by then. Not much, but a little; obviously just enough. Pete and Tim got involved and somehow explained that I was just going through worst-case scenarios and somehow got my numbers flipped and other such nonsense. It was just enough subterfuge to allay her anger and keep me my job. Tim actually felt a little bad. He'd been in her crosshairs once too, but not as badly. He was bummed he'd missed it. From that day on, I was always prepared. I never went to a meeting without at least a few copies of the information that presented the numbers in a non-threatening way that would make Kathy happy. A ridiculous way to work, but you know what they say—*when in Rome…*

29
HOW DID THIS HAPPEN?

My nine lives with the company, while surprising, also covered up something I had been refusing to acknowledge. I was now an accountant. Not really a CPA-like certified accountant. But I worked in finance and spent all day with numbers. For all intents and purposes I was an accountant. Since taking the job in finance I had devoted myself to being a good employee and moving up the corporate ladder. I added more and more suits to my wardrobe. I took to carrying a briefcase back and forth to the office. I got to work early. I stayed late. I was becoming a pretty darn good employee. But still, I was an accountant. *How the hell did I let this happen?*

For a while I had been fiddling with the idea that I wanted to be a writer or at least be doing something creative. Now I was spending all my time with spreadsheets and budgets. I wasn't happy, but I really didn't think I had any alternatives. I did try to pursue a writing career on the side, but after just a few rejections from *Esquire* and the like, I gave up that seemingly futile dream. I had a college degree in psychology, which wasn't really going to get me anywhere. It was totally useless now since I had no interest in that field. I also had no interest in the field I was in. The allure of working at a national magazine that I so eagerly jumped at when I was twenty-two seemed like it would eventually lead to something I wanted to do with my life. It did not. It led me to a small cramped office where I spent way too much time calculating numbers and analyzing budgets for a company that was quickly running out of money.

I had periods of utter depression due to the realization that I was a glorified accounting hack. Unfortunately, I was also *good* at being a glorified accounting hack. I now had a closet full of suits, a briefcase full of spreadsheets and carried around a calculator everywhere I went. The better I got at my job, the better the money got and that seemed to take the edge off. At some point, I figured I might as well just keep doing a good job and make as much as I could before the inevitable demise of this train wreck. I got as good as the others at spinning horseshit into gold. I learned to work the system like a champ. Kathy saw only the bright side of the business and the rest of us played a never-ending shell game to try to keep the place afloat.

30
BAR JACK

At this point you may be wondering whatever happened to dear old Jack, my college buddy who got me into this sticky little mess in the first place. Once Jack made his big move to advertising as a copywriter, he learned something very important. He didn't want to be a copywriter. That biz is all about writing and rewriting and everybody gets a say in what goes into the final creative product and that really wasn't Jack's thing. He was guy who liked to work solo. He believed in his work and didn't like seeing it mucked around with by others. His short stint in advertising frustrated him to no end.

He was one of those guys I clicked well with after college and then drifted away from. There was no specific reason. Looking back, I now know that this happens all the time. Sometimes all you need is proximity and a few things in common to be the best of friends. Jack and I had gone to the same college and lived next to each other in Stamford during that crucial time at the start of this story. Then we worked together for well over a year, commuting together and being as close as two guys get. Then he left the company, and proximity decreased. We still hung, out but less and less. We were both still part of the same college circle, but times change and people drift.

I then started spending more time with him around the time my corporate stock was rising. He and another college buddy had decided to open up a bar together and I was one of the few guys they knew with experience in the biz. So I spent a lot of time helping them plan out their big business. When they started gathering investors, I still didn't have enough disposable income to invest in a bar, but my time helping them earned me one important right—I got the Friday night bartending shift.

This made a huge change in my disposable income. In addition to the bigger bucks I was making at *Penthouse*, I was now making three to four hundred in cash every Friday night. Plus, it gave me a rush. Where I was feeling like a buttoned-up financial type around the office, now I was able to socialize, flirt and get drunk, all while making some coin.

I kept that Friday night shift for quite a while. I was the responsible corporate guy Monday through Friday, working a fifty-hour week, but when Friday night came, I would scoot downtown and bartend until 4am at No Idea (*it's still there at 30 East 20th Street—go visit!*).

Eventually, I started making enough dough at *Penthouse* that I really didn't need to keep bartending on Friday nights for extra cash, so I let my shift go to someone who needed it more. All it really did was free me up to go the other side of the bar, drink and meet girls. Pretty much the same thing I was doing from behind the bar but now with the allure that if I hit it off with someone I could actually skip out in the middle of the night to try to close the deal. This did not happen very often, but not unlike playing the lottery, you gotta play to win.

The fact that the bar continued to do well was always a safety net in the back of my mind. If I did lose my job, I now knew that at the very least I could pick up a few bartending shifts and scrape up a living. This, more than anything, was probably why when things at *Penthouse* got crappy, I could handle it with a sense of "Oh well, everything will work out." Without knowing I could make money at the bar, I'm sure I would have been a lot less cavalier.

31
HOWARD STERN

As my months of number-crunching turned into years, the one thing that got me through most days was the few hours I'd sit in my office every morning, drinking coffee and listening to Howard Stern on the radio. Starting my day laughing along to Howard and the gang made my job just a little bit easier. And on one of the more amusing mornings of that time, these two worlds collided.

But allow me to lay a little groundwork—in the early nineties, in the face of declining newsstand sales, the powers that be made a decision to put actual celebrities on the cover of *Penthouse*, instead of the usual generic models that had been the norm for decades. They started with a few specially shot covers of George Burns, Andrew Dice Clay and Dudley Moore posing with one of our Pets. Then for some reason, they tried a few more newsworthy covers. The first was Jerry Brown. *Jerry effing Brown!* It looked like a bad *Newsweek* cover. Then came a George Bush cover. It was a bizarre photo of him wearing a pig snout. As you can imagine, this led to quite a bit of reader backlash. Bob and the editors may have been proud of the political discourse in the pages of the magazine over the years, but the bulk of the *Penthouse* audience wasn't turning to the magazine for wry political discourse.

I get what they were trying to do—in theory, regular *Penthouse* readers would pick it up regardless of what was on the cover, because we were still offering the goods inside. With the divergent cover images they were hoping to attract new people. But it's a fine line to walk. Having a politician on the cover may or may not get you any new readers, but there certainly wouldn't be any unfulfilled expectations. Where they ran into trouble was when they put Cindy Crawford on the cover. She was still in the rarefied air of supermodel status and readers obviously assumed that if Cindy Crawford was on the cover of *Penthouse*, there was going to be a pictorial or at least some Cindy Crawford nudity featured in that issue. They were wrong. It was a classic bait and switch. The cover shot of her in lingerie was a stock image from a photo shoot that they bought on the cheap (truth be told, it wasn't even that good of a shot!). Reader backlash was palpable. And Crawford's camp wasn't too happy about it either.

They then chose my favorite cover from that period when they decided to do a feature on Howard Stern. Finally, a subject that was perfect for our audience!

I thought Howard was the perfect cover draw for the magazine, plus I was a huge fan. This was during his peak days in the early '90s when he was really on top of his game. It seemed like ideal synergy (see I was even starting to sound like a corporate guy!), since he often featured *Penthouse* Pets as guests on his show. Obviously, our material and the girls were right up his alley. And on several occasions, as I mentioned earlier, he'd have Bob himself on to talk about a special issue or Pet of the Year thing we were doing. I was a mundane cog in the wheel at that point, but it was cool to hear my workplace talked about on my favorite show.

The cover story inside the issue was actually a really good interview with Howard. His media profile at the time was incredible. He was syndicated in huge markets throughout the country, was a frequent guest on David Letterman's show and was in the process of writing his first book, *Private Parts*, that would be released the following year. So the *Penthouse*/Howard connection seemed like the perfect pairing. Until it actually hit the newsstands. For some reason they made a very odd choice for the cover blurb. They had a great shot of Howard in a leather jacket, his purple shirt complimenting the *Penthouse* logo perfectly. And right there next to Howard's face in bold type was the line "Howard Stern Has a Very Small Penis." *What the hell?* Granted, Howard had often commiserated on his show that he hadn't been blessed in the genital department. If I remember correctly, he usually explained that he was of completely average size, but when compared to his unusually tall frame, he felt he had been a little short-changed. His using it as a self-deprecating bit on his own show was one thing, but having it proclaimed on the cover of a huge national magazine was something else altogether. Especially a magazine that he'd championed for so long.

The morning the magazine hit the newsstand, he discussed his displeasure on his show. As the morning wore on, he got more and more worked up. Sitting there in my dingy little office, I loved that the magazine that was in my hand was the cause of such comical consternation on Howard's part. He worked himself into a tizzy. Finally, he got sick of just complaining about it and ordered his producer to get our art director on the phone.

I was sitting in my little office giggling my ass off at what was happening on the Stern show. He's yelling to get *Penthouse* on the phone. Suddenly, I heard the art director being paged over the intercom system. It was a great moment. Throughout the field of cubicles outside my door, you could tell the people who were listening to the show, because everyone stood up and laughed and couldn't wait to see how this was going to play out. All of the art offices were down on the second floor and I could only imagine the scrambling that must have been going on down there. It was surreal.

On the radio, Howard's producer was explaining that he was trying to get us on the phone and again I heard a much more urgent call over the office intercom to for him to return to his office. I never found out if he was actually in the office or just hiding from the call, but he never got on. But his deputy art director did. Howard railed at they guy, and rightfully so. He'd pimped our book and Bob's projects for years and we'd made him look like an idiot on our cover. Of course, that misstep did nothing to deter Howard's career and he eventually had the last laugh on our entire company.

32
RING-RING

In late 1992 we were starting to realize that one of our minor profit centers was really starting to take off—our phone sex division.

The home video market made porn readily available to the mass market. That and the endless addition of competitive titles on the newsstand had made *Penthouse* much less vital than it had been in the '70s and '80s. The brand still had a certain cachet, but the kingdom was crumbling. The phone sex boom seemed like it might be the saving grace. A few phone sex line advertisements in the back of the book generated so much revenue that they were quickly spawning many, many more. There were soon dozens and dozens of ads for various services, all of them making money at an incredible profit margin.

Our telecommunications operation was all run by a guy named Phil who had an office up on our underused fourth floor. I interacted with Phil the Phone Guy only when I was putting budgets together, but he seemed like a decent-enough guy. He seemed to fly under the radar. Now that the phone biz was turning a tremendous profit, more folks wanted to get their hands on it. Our CFO Pete had a meeting with Phil that raised some questions about how he was running things. Pete thought he was less than forthcoming with his answers, so he charged Tim and I with finding out more about the division.

The phone sex industry was coming of age at the exact right time. It was just before the Internet revolution—soon all manner of porn would be available to anyone with access to the World Wide Web and phone sex would lose its allure. But at the dawn of the '90s, the only way to get some safe female interaction from the comfort of your own home was through phone sex.

We were running two kinds of phone sex lines, live and recorded. For the recorded session, a customer could call the number and for ninety-nine cents a minute listen to a recording of a woman talking dirty. Then there were the live sessions that ran several dollars more per minute but put you in touch with real live women. The ads for these services always featured lusty, buxom women who looked exactly like the women in the pictorials in the rest of the magazine, creating the illusion that it is these lovely women that you would be talking to live. In reality, you were connected to a call center, usually out West, where rows of women were seated at identical cubicles wearing headsets and engaging in dirty chat. At a glance you would think it was a typical call center for a mundane mail-order house, except for all the naughty talk and moaning. Needless to say, these women did not look like the women in the ads. They were quite the opposite, mostly unattractive women who happened to have a knack for conversation. Since the customers were paying by the minute, the phone women were rewarded for keeping the customers on for extended periods of time. They even had a tote board at the front of the room that tallied who was best at getting customers to rack up the highest charges.

The pre-recorded business wasn't as profitable, but was easier to run. Up on the fourth floor, there was a small closet-sized office, not that different than mine, which had been soundproofed and converted into a recording studio. Phil had one freelancer he would bring in to record the taped sessions. She was a struggling actress who had found the perfect gig. She would come in and read the dirty scripts and never have to interact with any customers. Even though she was extremely talented and recorded them in any number of voices and dialects, she would also bring in a few of her actress friends to expand the library.

A typical script for one of these recorded sessions would go like this.

"Hello. Oh, it's you. Hi. I'm so glad you called. I was just thinking of you! I was just about to take a bath. Do you want to join me? Great! Come here help me slip out of these clothes. Ahhhhh, that's better. Do you like what you see? Okay your turn. Oh my! This IS going to be fun!"

And on and on it would go. Obviously the purpose of these calls was for the customer to get aroused and, you know, pleasure himself to completion. This was another business I really did not understand. I got the allure of dirty pictures to kind of get the ball rolling, but it seems like all you need is a little bit of an imagination to finish the deed on your own. I couldn't imagine having to hear a voice over the phone to get me there, especially when it cost a small fortune. But there were plenty of guys out there who dug it. We were making millions from our lines and we weren't the only game in town. Lots of money was being made back then off of lonely men with a phone in one hand and a box of tissues in the other.

As Tim and I learned more about the biz and how Phil had set up our phone division, we started to think Pete was right, maybe

Phil was hiding something. This led to my first case of corporate espionage. Again it was a silly little assignment, but way more exciting than my usual spreadsheet analysis.

Phil was slow to respond to our requests to see the partnership deals he'd put together for all of *Penthouse's* phone sex lines. Basically they were outsourced to outside partners and managed by Phil. Pete and Tim really wanted to see the deals he had put together so they sent me on a spy mission. They wanted me to sneak into his office and look for the contracts. I was a little concerned that I was doing something illegal, but they assured me that since he was a company employee, his office and all its belongings were subject to inspection. It sounded reasonable to me, but in hindsight, if it was that simple, why didn't they just go investigate it themselves?

They gave me a key to his office and I waited until almost seven o'clock at night. First I called his office twice and got no response. Then I called one of the security guys down in the lobby and said I couldn't find Phil and was wondering if he had left for the day. They assured me that they'd seen him heading out at about six. That meant the coast was clear. Or clear-ish. The fourth floor was sort of a hodgepodge of different employees and consultants in cubicles and offices, so I wasn't sure who would be working late or just roaming around.

Despite Pete and Tim's assurances that I wasn't doing anything wrong, I still had a pretty good case of nerves going. I tried my best to look nonchalant as I strolled the halls. I walked past Phil's closed office door once and didn't see anyone around. I could hear people on the phone and talking in other areas, but none were in sight. I circled back around and quickly unlocked the door, slipped inside and closed it shut again. It took maybe three seconds but my heart was pounding out of my chest.

I stood there in the dark listening intently. What for? I don't know. Phil worked alone. It's not like he had a crew of thugs lying in wait for someone to break into his office before they pounced on the would-be intruder and smashed him to smithereens. I caught my breath there in the dark and realized I was just being silly. I was in his office. All I had to do was find the files and head out. I was back on track, but I still didn't want to turn on the light. I had come prepared with a flashlight. I switched it on and started my search. My spy skills left something to be desired. Searching for stuff in the dark with a flashlight looks a lot easier in movies than it is in real life. Trying to go through his stuff without leaving any proof I was there was impossible. I kept knocking into things. Stuff slid off his desk. It was getting ugly. I stood still and gathered myself again. I decided that I should just turn on the small desk light, that way I could see better and get the job done quicker. I put the flashlight down and reached for the pull chain on the lamp. Then something quite unexpected happened.

Remember how I said earlier that I liked to gamble? By this point I was gambling pretty much every day. When I read the paper in the morning I would circle my picks for the night's games and wait to call them into Champ the security guard/bookie. Sometimes the lines changed so it was best to wait until right before game time. Since I was such an OCD gambler I was afraid I would miss the early games that started at 7:00 PM some nights, so I always had the timer set on my cheap Timex to go off at 6:50 PM every night to remind me to get my bets in. I, of course, had forgotten about this as I rummaged through Phil's office that night and reached for his light at exactly 6:54 and 59 seconds. Just as I clicked the lamp on, my watch started beeping.

Loudly. It didn't seem that loud the other 364 days of the year, but tonight it sounded like a friggin' smoke alarm. My first reaction was to turn the light off right away. My brain knew that turning the light on didn't cause the beeping, but it was pure instinct. I pulled the chain too quickly and the lamp toppled over.

I hit what I thought was the button on my watch to turn off the alarm, but in the dark, I must have hit the wrong one. Panicked, I fumbled for the flashlight. I couldn't quite shine the light on my wrist and figure out the right button at the same time and the flashlight ended up squirting out of my hand and clanking loudly against the metal filing cabinet. With the beam of light stretched across the floor, I quickly took a knee and was able to silence my alarm. I stayed there for a minute. I was dripping with sweat at this point and ready to abandon my mission. But from my vantage point I could see that one of the metal file drawers was open a few inches. I slid it open and found exactly what I was looking for. I grabbed it and made a run for it. As I slipped out of his office, there was still no one in sight.

I went back downstairs and proudly presented the file to Tim. "Great. Make copies of everything, then put it back where you found it."

I had to go back in there?

I took a few minutes to recover from the excitement upstairs. And to call in my bets to Champ.

GAMBLING SIDE NOTE

Looking back now, I'm pretty sure that in a real corporation, my high stakes gambling with another employee would have been big trouble. Especially now that I was high up on the financial ladder of the company. I was able to approve lots of expenses and they could easily assume that I might be compromised to take advantage of my position. Not at *Penthouse*. Even Pete, the head of Finance, knew what I was up to. During March Madness when they played big college basketball games during work hours, he'd let me keep track of the games in his office since he was the only one with a TV. I would think he should have been alarmed at one of his employee's obvious gambling addiction (*especially when his bookie was another employee who sat a hundred feet away with a loaded gun!*) It never seemed to bother Pete. His only real involvement was a *schadenfreude* reaction whenever I'd lose a close one. He'd always let out a nasty little cackle when I'd lose a game at the buzzer. It amused the shit out of him.

Once I'd called in what I'm sure ended up being losing bets to Champ, I made copies and returned Phil's file. The second trip was much less disastrous. I just opened the door and with the light from the hallway was able to slip the file back where I found it, close the drawer and be on my way. It only took a few moments and I was heading back downstairs to review the contracts I'd swiped.

After a formal review by Pete, Tim and the lawyers, the general consensus was that Phil *might* have been skimming from the business. Every deal he made was a 50/50 split, which didn't make a lot of sense since we were the bigger company and providing all of the advertising. They assumed that Phil had rigged the deal in favor of the vendors and was probably getting a kickback under the table. Since there was no smoking gun evidence in the files I'd copied, they decided to set up a meeting where they would ask him to explain the deals we'd uncovered and hope to trip him up on his scheme. The lawyers thought it best to stay out of the meeting since they didn't want to put Phil on guard, so they said the best thing to do was secretly record the conversation, that way if he slipped and admitted his misdealings we'd have him dead to rights.

Pete and Tim called in Giancarlo. He was the head of the security team and he spent the majority of his time over at Bob and Kathy's house. The only time I'd see him was when he came in for budget meetings. These get-togethers with the department heads were extremely boring exercises in going over how much each department spent, discussing how much would be allotted to them next year, etc. But meetings with Giancarlo were different. There weren't a lot of variables. He had his team of ex-cops on staff and their expenses were minimal. At most, he'd haggle for a few more bucks for bullets so his guys could stay sharp on the range. The bulk of our time was Giancarlo telling us stories about being on the force. Compared to discussing travel expenses with a sales rep, hearing him tell stories about shooting perps and guys getting knifed in the belly was an entertaining little part of the process.

Giancarlo, the former cop, was an imposing guy, but not the type I would turn to for covert technical work.

He said he'd come by the next day with a secret recording device. He showed up with a secret pen recorder that looked more like a kid's toy. He tried to show us how it worked, but had some difficulty. When he finally got it going we realized that it only worked if the pen was a few inches from a person's mouth. In a pocket from across a conference table, the recording was unintelligible. We thanked Giancarlo for his work and went with Plan B.

Plan B was Tim and I going to The Secret Spy Shop, a store in Manhattan that specialized in surveillance and spy gear. We bought a tiny, high-density microphone with a thin cord that could be connected to a Walkman-like tape recorder. The only problem was that it would be pretty obvious if the little recorder were whirring away in the corner of the room. When we got back to the office, I planted the microphone inside a plant on a side table in the conference room and ran the wire through the wall to the office next door. We tested it out and we were able to pick up voices from any spot in the room. The plan was that Tim and Pete would confront Phil in there and I would be in the next room working the recorder.

The next day I sat in the corner of that office with headphones on and an assortment of extra tapes and backup batteries in case the meeting went long. They didn't want anyone to know what we were up to so I couldn't tell the woman whose office it was what I was doing. She sat silently at her desk while I huddled next to the wall, listening intently to my headphones and taking notes.

After all that drama, I wish I could say there was a major confrontation, an admission of guilt and endless scandal. There was no such thing. What it boiled down to was that Bob had put Phil in charge of the biz a few years prior with the one caveat: Don't put too much capital at risk. It was the first time I'd heard of him being fiscally responsible!

So Phil went out and made deals where we advertised certain sex lines and the vendors covered the production costs and everybody made a fair penny. No shenanigans, no horseplay. Poor Phil was pretty insulted that they thought he was being less than upfront with them. Imagine how insulted he would have been if he'd known the kid listening in on his conversation in the room next door had snuck into his office and violated his personal space. And possibly broken his lamp.

Even though no impropriety had been found, Pandora's box had been opened. We now knew how much money was to be made in the phone sex trade, so eventually Phil was edged out, all deals with the vendors were rescinded and we took more control of the enterprise in an attempt to get a bigger piece of the pie.

This actually worked out incredibly well for me. Since this new telecommunications division had such huge potential as a profit center, they put Tim in charge of the whole operation. This meant they were promoting me to Budget Director! At the ripe old age of twenty-eight I was the budget director for a multi-million dollar international publishing empire. Not too shabby.

My promotion came with a new office. It wasn't big, but it had a window. I was moving up in the world once again. After my testy dust-up with Kathy in front of a room full of people a few years earlier, I'd gotten back in her good graces. I got to hire my replacement. I got more money. Things were looking pretty good. Most importantly, by this point, I was actually really good at my job. I worked well with all the department heads as we all tried our best to keep the ship a' rolling.

33
PENTHOUSE COMIX

One day Tim asked me to sit in on a meeting with him. He didn't give me a lot of details, but that wasn't so unusual. We both worked pretty well together so whatever it was I knew I could handle it. I'll admit, this one caught me a little off-guard. Into his office walked a big bear of a man. At the time, I had just finished reading John Kennedy Toole's *A Confederacy of Dunces*, a great book about a guy named Ignatius J. Reilly, a delusional eccentric who also happens to be sloppily disheveled hulking lout. As I sat in one of Tim's chairs I thought this guy was Ignatius J. Reilly brought to life. For a second I thought, *I must have mentioned to Tim that I was reading that book and he brought this guy into play a prank on me.* This was no prank.

Tim introduced himself. "Hi, I'm Tim nice to meet you. This is our budget director, Steve."

I extended my hand and it was quickly enveloped by a large, sweaty meathook.

"George Caragonne. Nice to meet you." He took a seat and I noticed right away that the sweat on his hands was just the tip of the iceberg; he was a sweaty, drippy mess. It didn't help that he had a scarf wrapped around his neck on a warm spring day. He was clearly dressed to play the role of artiste.

"Thank you for meeting me today, gentlemen. I had such a lovely chat with Bob and Kathy at the party last weekend. It's great to talk to people who get my ideas." And right away I knew what was going on. Bob and Kathy were constantly inundated by people pitching them projects—dreamers looking for funding for the Next Big Thing. I'm not sure if Guccione was seen as an easy mark, but he did seem to gravitate towards the most outlandish ideas. Occasionally, these persistent folks would be granted an innocuous meeting with the finance department that would go nowhere. Tim handled more of these than I did, but I had sat in enough of them to know just to listen to whatever the pitch was and get the guy out in a timely manner without giving him the feeling he was being brushed off.

George explained that he was a comic book writer and that he had many successes at Marvel and Valiant Comics. He had been introduced to Bob and Kathy and pitched them the idea of some 1960s comic he gotten the rights to and was hoping to revise. I had never heard of the old comic, but watching an ex-Marvel guy sweat his way through a pitch was better entertainment than working on boring spreadsheets in my office, so he had my attention.

"Bob didn't seem too interested in funding my idea," he said. "But he really wanted to find a way to work with me." He drew that out like it was obvious that anyone would want to work with the great George Caragonne. All I really wanted to do was grab that damn sweater from around his neck and wipe the river of sweat sliding down the side of his face.

"So, Bob asked me if I'd be willing to write some new comics to run in *Penthouse*. Wholly original stuff," he continued. I turned to Tim and silently asked, "Really?" He just shrugged his shoulders. He looked like he just wanted to get this big guy out of his office. I assumed George would now tell us how much it would cost for him to put a few pages of comics together and we could wrap things up and never have to deal with him again.

Then George reached into his bag and pulled out his real proposal. He wanted to do more than just a few pages in the magazine. He wanted to start a whole new comic book line.

"We'll call it *Penthouse Comix*. With an X! And I'll be able to get the best artists in here and the books will be filled with wondrous stories and the most voluptuous women ever committed to paper! It will be a smashing success!!"

This was his big reveal, his magic moment, and Tim and I responded with utter confusion. Then we hit him with a barrage of questions.

"Like a kid's comic book? With the *Penthouse* name on it?" asked Tim.

"No! It will be strictly for adults."

"So it will be dirty?" I asked.

"Not dirty. *Sexy!*"

"So a comic book full of naked women?" asked Tim.

"Not just naked women. *Beautiful* naked women. And doing the most *erotic* things!"

We went back and forth like that for a while. Admittedly, neither Tim nor I were comic biz aficionados, but this just didn't make sense to us. We didn't think there'd be a market out there for such a product. Dirty comic books for adults? Why not just buy a regular *Penthouse* and get the real thing?

The kicker was when he presented his big tag line. You could tell how proud he was because he paused and presented it with a grand flourish.

"*Penthouse Comix*, the comics you read with one hand."

It took us a second to get the implied meaning that you'd be using your other hand to pleasure yourself, but he seemed over the moon proud with the business opportunity he had just laid on us. Tim, ever the professional, complimented him on his pitch and assured him we'd be in touch.

Once he was gone, we finally acknowledged the ridiculousness of the whole thing. Neither one of us thought there was a market for the product, but we both agreed that he seemed more like a *Saturday Night Live* character than a businessman. We giggled for a few minutes and went back to work.

Imagine my surprise a week later when Tim called me back into his office and there was George Caragonne once again. He didn't seem quite as nervous this time, and for good reason. Bob had ignored the advice from Tim and I and had decided to stake George as the co-founder of *Penthouse Comix*. It was now up to Tim and I to set up this guy with a new company, a working budget, office space, etc. I was stunned. *This is a guy they decided to stake?*

If you think I was harsh in my description of him before, trust me, I was not. This guy was a buffoonish blowhard that I would not have trusted with the smallest of projects and now they were giving him a small fortune to hire a staff and launch a brand new comics company. At a time when we should have been battening down the hatches and trying to ride out the recent wave of financial downfalls. But, again, that was the beauty of Bob G.—he was not a man afraid to take chances. He had swung for the fences as a young man and hit a grand slam, so even now, if he believed in an idea, he went in whole hog.

The problem was that we now had to make this whole comics idea work. There was trouble right away. George quickly hired a staff and started spending money like crazy. The nervous guy that sweated through that first pitch in Tim's office quickly became a mini-tyrant. He thought that since he had Bob's blessing, he could run his own show however he saw fit. He became a petulant child when we questioned any of his expenses or opposed one of his grand ideas. *Did I need this headache?*

Eventually, we had to move on to dealing with more pressing problems with the other books and left the comics division to fend for themselves. Until one morning when one of the security guys came to me saying there was a problem over in the Comix department. It was early in the morning and I was the highest-ranking guy around. I wandered over and, sure enough, was shocked at what I found. The area stunk of pot smoke. They had a bullpen area with some couches gathered around and there was a guy sound asleep on one of them with a few beer bottles strewn about. It looked like the party room of a frat house, not a division of a multi-million-dollar publishing company. Inside George's office there was a huge bookcase full of movies on videocassette. It looked like the wall of a Blockbuster, with rows of endless movies that he bought with company money. (*Kids, ask your folks to explain what a videocassette and Blockbuster are.*) He later explained that they were for research because his Comix were going to be so tuned in to pop culture. It also turned out that the sleeping figure was a freelancer and not even a real employee. He should not have had access to the building after hours, let alone be passed out in a weed- and booze-induced haze.

I quickly decided that this situation was above my pay grade and I told the security guy to tell his boss Giancarlo. This was a matter for the guys with the guns to resolve. And I was right. By the end of the day, they had turned up illegal narcotics on the premises, a few staff members had been let go and George had been put on notice. *Penthouse Comix* was hardly off the ground and already there was serious trouble.

Bob must have had a word with George about the incident, because he seemed to right the ship after that. We pumped out issues of *Penthouse Comix* and even produced one of *Omni Comix*. They weren't a failure, but they certainly didn't set the world on fire. In my eyes, they were not worth the time and money invested, but they kept chugging along.

Eventually, George started reverting back to his old ways. There were lots of questions about his spending and he ended up being accused of mishandling company funds. Of course, the whole place ran on a culture of mishandling company funds, but he went too far, taking a little too much advantage of Bob's largesse. There was quite a bit of drama when they finally let George go. He did not go without a fight. He ranted and raved and tilted at windmills. What I did not know was that George was a deeply disturbed individual with a severe drug dependency.

The sad conclusion to this story is that George committed suicide in a truly horrific fashion by jumping from the 45th floor of a midtown hotel, to the absolute terror of nearby tourists. The drugs, being fired and the failure of his Comix dream were too much for him too handle.

My bookie stopped by my office to tell me the morning after it happened. I felt horrible, but I thought back to that first meeting and I had known right off the bat that this guy wasn't someone to get involved with, and yet the company had welcomed him in. Something about this place was a magnet for misfits, from the collection of oddballs that worked there to the people who gravitated towards Bob with their crazy ideas, all the way back to the young naïve kid that was me who jumped at a job here without a second's hesitation. Something was drawing us all in. *Was there ever a way to get out?*

34
FINALLY MEETING BOB

By this point, I'd worked there for almost seven years and still had yet to meet Bob Guccione. But my time had finally come. I was invited to a budget meeting at "The House," Bob's multi-million dollar residence on the Upper East Side of Manhattan. It was a five-story townhouse across the street from where Nixon used to live. (*I wonder if Tricky Dick ever popped over to borrow a cup of sugar?*) It was actually two townhouses that Bob had had bought, knocking down the dividing wall and creating an impressive mansion in the heart of Manhattan.

Like my first meeting with Kathy years before, where Tim had prepped me on how to behave, Pete, the CFO, told me exactly what to do. I was to keep my answers brief. I was not to offer up any information not asked of me, but I was supposed to tell the truth when asked. It sounded like he was prepping me for a jury deposition more than a business meeting.

By this time the folks above me were determined to convince Bob just how much trouble the company was in. It was impossible to ignore. I still don't think he was fazed by it. I assumed he either refused to believe it or that by that point he had heard rumblings of "the sky is falling" so many times that he assumed that things would work themselves out as they always had before. And recently things had perked up ever so slightly. The phone sex biz had become a huge influx of cash that helped out greatly, but even with that huge new revenue stream it was obvious that he could not keep losing millions on *Omni* and *Longevity*. The future of those two books was what this meeting was really about, and it had been purposefully planned for a day when Kathy was out of town.

Pete had an earlier meeting with Bob, so he was already at the House when I arrived for the first time. I found the address and knocked on the ornately heavy door. It was opened by one of the ever-present guards in brown poly sports coats. He checked my name on his list and let me in, leading me through a medieval-looking foyer. As I walked, I glanced to my left and was shocked to look through a door to see a gold-lined swimming pool shimmering in the dark light. Of course I knew there was an indoor pool, mostly because I'd been signing off on bills for its upkeep for years, but I just didn't expect it to be right there by the entrance. We kept walking and he led me to one of the living rooms. He explained that they were just finishing up another meeting and someone would come get me soon enough. He turned to leave, then paused for a moment. "The pooches will be back from their walk soon and they'll be wandering about. You okay with that?" the guard asked.

I like dogs, so I said it was fine with me. Plus, I was curious to meet the dogs whose semen-storage bills I'd been approving for years. He walked back to his post as I sank uncomfortably into the horribly unsupportive leather couch. *What is it with these people?*

Can't they buy a normal couch? I sat there awkwardly with my legs up under my chin for quite a while. I heard a ruckus somewhere in the House and hoped that meant that Bob was finally ready for me. He wasn't.

What I heard was tough to decipher, such a strange sound. Then it hit me. It was the clickety-clack of claws on the fine Italian floor tiles. *Here come the dogs,* I thought. But I was wrong. These weren't normal dogs. They were as big as small horses. And not ponies either. These "pooches" looked like they could eat a pony for dinner. Again, I knew about the dogs, but to be confronted by them in an empty room was momentarily terrifying. And, of course, they could smell my fear. They both stood staring at me. Between their height and the lowness of the couch, we were all at the same eye level. One briefly snarled and bared his teeth, causing me to flinch, before turning away and trotting off uninterested. But not the other one. He was very interested. I thought he was being friendly when he came over towards me. Perhaps he just wanted me to give him a pat on the head. He bypassed my outstretched hand and instead buried his head in my crotch like a pig looking for buried truffles. I wasn't scared, because he was doing it so affectionately, but I was still put off by this huge animal burying his cinder block of a noggin in my lap. While trying to fend off his amorous advances, a young woman appeared at the bottom of the stairs to say, "They're ready for you upstairs." *Of course they were.* Upon hearing her voice, the dog lost interest in me and trotted off down the hall.

I collected myself, stood and grabbed my briefcase. Upon standing, I realized that in the act of burying his head in my crotch, the dog had left a copious amount of dog spit and slime on my pants. As the lovely young woman led me up the stairs on my first trip to the *Penthouse* mansion, I did my best to cover the huge wet stain that graced the front of my trousers. Just liked I'd always imagined it.

I was led to a large dining room, again with a medieval theme and a large, wooden Camelot-like table. There were six other folks there, all high-level department heads that I knew from the office. We all made small talk as we took our seats. I pulled my binders and stuff out of my briefcase as I wondered when the man himself would be making his big entrance. I was startled by a hand over my right shoulder and that deep, soulful voice. "I'm Bob, I don't believe we've met." And there he was. I shook his hand as Pete introduced us. "It's a pleasure to meet you, Mr. Guccione." And it really was. For all the craziness of the company and my ridiculous dealings with his wife, this guy was still a huge figure in the publishing industry and pop culture history. Plus, that deep baritone of his was still in full force and instantly commanded respect. "Call me Bob," he said as he smiled and sat at the head of the table.

Right away I could tell we were off to a good start. Bob seemed aware of the dire circumstances of his wife's two pet projects. Unlike my dealings with Kathy, this seemed like a real meeting. We all contributed various ideas, possible solutions. It seemed every cost-cutting solution was on the table, right down to the possibility of shuttering both mags. As I sat there in this elaborate mansion, having these high-end financial discussions, I started to think things might turn out all right. Bob seemed to have a good grasp of the situation and maybe he could pull a rabbit out of the hat again, stop wasting money and turn *Penthouse* back into the profitable empire it once was. At this point, Pete asked Bob directly, "Do you want us to shut *Omni* down?"

The room fell silent as Bob contemplated the fate of his wife's crown jewel. A business school student would have looked at the books and shut it down in an instant. A wise man would have shut it down a decade ago. A loving husband would have shut it down when its losses became overwhelming. But Bob sat and thought. We all just stared and waited. I took him in. He sat there in jeans and a velour pullover shirt unzipped two inches too low for a man his age, but the thick swath of chest hair still stood there as a testament to his virility. His hair was intriguing. I'd seen him in photos and from afar and his hair looked perfectly normal, but here, up close, something wasn't quite right. It looked like that terrible toupee Burt Reynolds used to wear in the '80s. Hell, it might have been the same exact hairpiece Burt wore in the '80s. What better thing to purchase for a man whose manhood was so important? Or maybe he just had bedhead. It was true that he stayed up working and painting every night and slept during the day. I was sure he'd only just woken up recently for the earlier meeting with Pete. Even his skin, which always looked so tanned and vibrant in photos, had an unnatural tint to it.

I was trying to put it all together in my head while still envisioning a positive future for the company. Seeing that he was seriously contemplating the appropriate fiscal moves his situation required made me think that the company, and more importantly my career, were again on an upward swing.

Then he finally spoke. "Do I think we should shut down *Omni?*" followed by a long pause and a big sip from his can of Tab. "No. I don't think so. I think we just need to revitalize it!"

Okay, not the answer I was expecting, but at least he was going to make a change. There were any number of ideas that had been floated around before, like targeting a younger demographic, spending less on the iconic sci-fi art that Kathy loved but cost us a fortune, expanding the areas of science we covered. I'm not sure if any of them would have done the trick, but any change would probably help. Or so I thought.

"We need to ramp up the UFO coverage." *What?!* I was hoping I'd misheard that big baritone. Did he really say we needed more UFO coverage? As in flying saucers? We'd already covered them quite a bit, which had not done us any favors in the credible science community. Obviously, the rest of the room had heard the same thing because they were all trying to cover the same defeated look on their faces that I had.

"We need to expand our coverage. The government's UFO conspiracy is going to come crashing down on them at some point and we should be the ones to do it!" He then rambled on about the real existence of alien spaceships like an excited fourteen-year-old at a sleepover.

And that was the moment. For most of my career at *Penthouse*, I was convinced we were slowly heading down a doomed path, but was never 100 percent sure. For a few minutes earlier in the meeting I'd almost convinced myself that I'd been wrong and maybe Bob could once again lead us to success. Then he decided to take on the government's huge UFO conspiracy and I realized that, not only was the ship going down, but it was going down even quicker than I thought. To their credit, the rest of the execs listened intently as he rehashed old UFO stories and the meeting ended not with approval to make drastic financial cuts, but with the charge to go spend *more money* on a harebrained UFO exposé. As we walked down the stairs, Pete just chuckled at my dumbfounded reaction. These guys had heard these ramblings before, but this was my first day seeing how the sausages got made and I was not happy.

After years of working for the icon that was Bob Guccione, finally meeting him in the flesh made me think about who he really was. A few decades earlier, he'd been a regular guy just like me, looking to make his mark on the world. And, like me, he had dreams. He dreamed of being a painter and after taking a few detours he ended up with his own publishing house. He had more or less stumbled into his massive magazine career and now, twenty-five years later, he was still trying to figure things out. Was he that different than me? I had other dreams when I was younger but ended up following the path that led me to here. Working at a slowly dying company in an unfulfilling job and a career path I did not want.

UFO's aside, I couldn't really blame Bob for being out of his element any more than I could blame myself. We were all in this predicament together and none of us knew how it was going to turn out.

35
MO' MONEY,
MO' PROBLEMS

By 1994 the fiscal health of the place had become so bad that drastic changes had to be made. Outside financial experts were consulted and Bob and Kathy were talked into refinancing the whole corporation. The plan was to sell bonds to raise capital and right the ship. Consultants were brought in, all charging exorbitant fees, to put together the documents that would make the place look like a stable corporation, which it definitely was not. An endless supply of snappily dressed business school guys came in acting like the big swinging dicks they were. I gave them whatever they wanted, but was mostly left out of the loop. That was okay with me since I really did not want to participate in their charade.

They showed endless projections that made the company look like it would be a solvent powerhouse in just a year or two. Their numbers were more optimistically pie-in-the-sky than Kathy had ever dreamed of. But it worked. They got enough investors to buy in to actually keep things afloat. But they'd signed their own death penalty. With those bonds came huge interest payments. And by the time they came due, the business school guys with their briefcases full of fees and commissions were long gone. They ended up being the last of the shady shamans that would shake the few remaining shekels out of the *Penthouse* tree.

36
THE BEGINNING OF THE END
(STEVE THE HYPOCRITE)

I'm not proud of my behavior from that moment on. It's not that I went crazy and wrecked the joint. I did something even worse. I stopped caring. Before the UFO revelation, I hadn't loved my job, but I mostly wanted to be good at it. Afterwards, I kind of developed a "who cares" mentality. The ship was going down with me on it, so I could either cling to the handrails and pray for a miracle that would never come or I could grab my cello and play as the water came over the bow. And that's what I did. I chose the cello.

I didn't give up entirely, I just did as little as possible to cover up the fact that I didn't care anymore. I figured they'd catch on and finally get rid of me within a few weeks. They didn't. So I just went with the flow. I went from trying to be a diligent finance guy to just another guy in the office taking advantage of my situation.

I knew that people were taking advantage of the place, but it would be hypocritical of me not to admit that I benefitted as well. I was constantly entitled to perks that young finance guys should not have had access to. Like our fleet of cars. For some reason we had a fleet of leased cars that were kept in the parking garage below the building. Since so many folks lived in Manhattan and didn't own cars these were used for executives when they needed to make trips or for sales people who needed to travel the region to drum up some business. What they should not have been used for is a guy like me who liked to golf and get out of the city a lot. It was a hell of a perk once I was introduced to it.

Living in Manhattan without a car meant I was at the whim of train schedules to really venture anywhere outside of the subway system. Occasionally, me and the guys would rent a car to head down to Atlantic City for the weekend or venture to the suburbs for a day of golf. But that was a pricey extravagance. Now, all I had to do was call Carl, who was in charge of our fleet. If he had a spare car, and he always did, he'd stop by and toss me the keys. All I'd have to do is return it with a full tank of gas and I was good to go. Those cars took me all over. Trips to Atlantic City, concerts out at Giants Stadium, even the occasional trip home to Massachusetts to see my family. It was an amazing perk, but one that as a finance guy I should have put an end to. There was no corporate reason for me to use a company car, and I bet if I dug a little deeper I'd find little reason to keep the whole fleet. But we had them, so I used them. *Hypocrite.*

Another corporate privilege were our season tickets to the Knicks. They were supposed to be used by the ad sales guys to woo clients, but for some reason they often went unclaimed. Pete's secretary was the person responsible for doling out the tickets. Since she liked me, she often offered them to me when they were available, which was quite often. I was living about fifteen blocks from Madison Square Garden at the time, so this was a real treat.

During the early 1990s I had great seats to most of the intense Bulls vs. Knicks playoff games. I got to watch Michael Jordan and Patrick Ewing face off in one of the greatest sports rivalries of the time. All on Bob Guccione's dime. *Hypocrite.*

I also had an expense account, which was absolutely ridiculous. I only interacted with company employees and never had any reason whatsoever to schmooze outside clients. Still, I had a company credit card and would rack up big lunch and Happy Hour tabs just because I could. *Hypocrite.*

These things may sound big, but in the grand scheme of things they were a small drip in the huge bucket of the ways that people had taken advantage of Bob Guccione and his *Penthouse* company over the decades. I'm not justifying what I did, but certainly these "perks" could be seen as a reasonable part of my compensation. They only amounted to a few thousand of dollars at most, as opposed to the millions upon millions that had been wasted, bilked and mismanaged by the company.

37
AND THE COUNTDOWN BEGINS

As 1994 was coming to a close I was still spending a lot of time at the bar and taking comfort in the fact that I always had my bartending safety net to fall back on. At work I was trying to balance my apathy with my desire to succeed. I'd go from working my ass off for two weeks straight, to not really caring about any of it. One day I'd decide to buckle down and focus on my career path, the next I'd be ready to toss it all away and bartend full time. Not a great mindset.

By this time my meetings with Kathy were no longer fraught with fear. I knew how to read her temperament a little better. I had the business side down cold and I knew how to present the numbers to her. At least I usually did. In the fall of 1994, as we prepared our budgets for the following year, I put together a number of scenarios for her pride & joy, *Omni Magazine*. As I've mentioned this odd hybrid of science-fiction and science-fact had never turned a profit since its premier issue in 1978. It had always been propped up by the *Penthouse* cash cow, but now that the mothership was starting to falter, something needed to be done.

We had yet to expand the UFO coverage that Bob thought would breathe some new life into the book, but none of us believed that would have any positive effect.

I had been down this road before, as had Tim before me along with I'm sure every budget director going back to 1978. We were always looking for ways to cut back and save a little money on this title that was hemorrhaging cash. Even Kathy knew it at this point. Something had to be done to improve *Omni's* bottom line.

So for this particular meeting I had my usual stack of info-filled binders in my hand and a simple three-page handout for Kathy to review. There were three different scenarios, each an attempt to improve the mag's bottom line. One proposed combining a few issues over the course of the year and only producing ten instead of twelve, thereby saving on manufacturing costs. Another scenario featured a change in the fancy paper stock we used to something more economical, a change she always rejected, but I kept proposing month after month. The third scenario had a few of the overly eager projections that she had mentioned in our last meeting. She was always optimistic about advertising revenue trends and newsstand sales increases. These were the three options we had, but I knew that only the first would work and, in fact, we were already planning on implementing those changes.

Then things got hairy. I guess I had gotten so comfortable in her presence that I may not have been paying the best attention. My mind wandered to a pretty new girl that Tim had hired in the ad services department. It had been ages since I'd asked out anyone in the office, but I wondered if she'd go out with me.

"That will work, won't it?" asked Kathy, shaking me out of my brief daydream.

I didn't know what she said, but I realized I had been blindly shaking my head in agreement while she rambled on. *Uh-oh? What do I say?*

"It will, won't it?" she asked again. This time the smile on her face was getting bigger.

Time to hedge.

"Well, it might, but we'll have to run the numbers a few more times," I said. *That should buy me a day or two.* But it didn't.

"No you've already done all the work. It's all here!"

Then she walked me through her plan. The plan that I had just blindly agreed would work. She somehow pulled various elements of all three plans together in a way that took all of the best assumptions and ignored the downsides. It was a plan that would never work. Except I just told her that it would.

"This is wonderful! Come with me." she said excitedly shaking my three-page handout. She stood up and headed out the door. I grabbed my cumbersome binders and rushed after her. I'll say this for her, when she got a full head of steam, she could really move on those six-inch stilettos. I didn't know where she was taking me. Then I figured it out, she was headed to Pete the CFO's office. *Well, this can't be good.*

Kathy burst in, with me stumbling behind. As luck would have it, Pete was in a meeting with Tim and they both took it in stride that Kathy was interrupting them with me in tow.

"Hello, Kathy, how are you doing today?" asked Pete smoothly.

"I'm great, now," she beamed.

The two of them looked at her expectedly.

"Stephen has done it. He's figured out a way to turn *Omni* profitable! Isn't that marvelous?"

Neither one of them looked at me right away.

Pete hid behind his poker face, "Oh, he has, has he? Yes, that is marvelous."

"I'll let him go over the details with you, but this is very exciting indeed." Then she turned on her heels and headed out, but not before pausing to give me the most earnest accolade she had ever bestowed. "Good job, Stephen. Very good work!"

I watched her walk out, mostly because I was too afraid to face Pete and Tim. When I finally did, I was not happy with the look in their eyes. I knew that look. I was a dead man walking. In a few simple minutes, I had dug myself a hole I could never escape. Kathy thought I was the knight in shining armor that was going to save her precious magazine. We all knew that was impossible. The simple fact was that *Omni* was dying a slow death. And now that she had appointed me its savior, I was doomed to follow the same fate.

I tried to explain. "It was a simple mistake! She just cherry-picked the best assumptions! Look, we can just…"

Pete put up his hand. "Tim and I have a few things to finish up here. We'll discuss this later." And that was that. I was excused.

I went back to my office and played over the events of the last few minutes in my head. I briefly thought back to the numerous times I'd been in this situation in my early days. But something was different. I still had that feeling like I'd screwed up and was about to be fired, but it didn't have the same effect. Instead of fear, I felt relief. Maybe it was time to go and this might be the push I needed.

After a while Tim came in. I assumed he'd just laugh off this debacle like he'd done many times in the past, but his face gave him away. He was distraught.

"What the hell did you do?" he asked like an upset father reprimanding a dumb teenager.

I told him about the three scenarios I presented and my momentary lack of concentration. He took it all in for a few moments. I was hoping he'd have some words of encouragement. But he just hung his head and said, "Well, I guess we just wait to see how it plays out."

And that's what we did. We prepared our budgets based on more realistic expectations, but Kathy didn't care. She already had it in her head that we were going to magically make *Omni* profitable, thanks to my special plan, and that was that. My fate was now tied to a failing book like a pirate chained to a sinking anchor. Back down into the depths for me.

A month later, as the holidays approached, Bob and Kathy were so thrilled they had secured the $80 million bond deal they were sure would save the company that they invited all of us finance folks who had worked on it to a party at the House. I wasn't nearly as intimidated as I had been the first time I went. To me this was just a work gathering where I could grab a few drinks and move on. I was actually hoping to get out of there pretty early because I had been fighting a nasty cold all week and just wanted to go to bed. I paid my dues for a while and thought I might be able to make my escape when Kathy corralled me for a private chat. She led me to a corner of the room because she had some new ideas she wanted to add to my special *Omni* plan.

Now here's where things got a little fuzzy. Between the din of the crowd mingling a few feet away, her hushed tones delivered in that high-pitched South African accent and my combining a few drinks with a day's worth of cold medicine, I could not understand a word she said. I kept asking her to repeat herself, but at a certain point I just gave up. I just pretended I knew what she was talking about and responded when it felt appropriate.

"Mumble mumble mumble subscriber base mumble mumble."

"Certainly," I'd nod.

"Advertising silly pants mumble eraser bibbles can't mumble tumble," she'd continue.

"Good point!"

"Mumblety mumble sassafrass dragon flaggin Saskatoon newsstand copies."

And so on.

Eventually she wrapped up and moved on. I quickly made my exit and went home to sleep off my cold. As I drifted off I tried to figure out how I was going to get out of this *Omni* pickle. The book was going down and there was no way to save it. Or me.

38
OOOH, SHE'S PRETTY

During the final week of 1994, an impromptu department outing occurred. Just one of those end-of-the-year things when everyone decided to go out to Happy Hour together. I joined in the festivities and ended up spending quite a bit of time with the pretty young woman I'd been daydreaming of in my meeting with Kathy that got me into so much trouble.

Her name was Kelly and I was instantly smitten. She was unbelievably cute, and so full of joy and laughter. She was more like the fresh-faced college girls I'd hung out with in my Connecticut days than the harder-edged New York women who had become my norm. We seemed to hit it off quite well, but apart from the obvious beer-infused chemistry, there were a few problems. First off, she had a boyfriend. *Not good.* Secondly, I had a girlfriend. *Even worse!* And finally, there was Howard's old adage about not dipping my pen in company ink. Kelly's department, in part, reported to me, so it would be quite out of line to ask out an underling.

Her having a boyfriend was the least of my troubles. The girl I was seeing at the time was just another in a long string of mediocre relationships I'd been involved with in the past few years. It wasn't her fault, or any of the other girls for that matter. It was me. My head wasn't in the right place. I was drinking a lot, gambling too much and couldn't decide if I wanted to be a corporate executive or a full-time bartender. This did not make me good boyfriend material.

As the night went on, I could tell there was a pretty deep connection to the lovely young Kelly. We never went beyond mild flirtation, but there was definitely something there. *Should I go for it?*

In the end, I held off. I told myself it was because I just didn't need to get myself into any more hot water at work, but deep down it was more because I knew that at the time, I was a bit of a mess and she seemed too nice to spoil with my raggedness. We never really saw each other outside of the office after that night, but I always enjoyed chatting with her in the halls. Just seeing her pass by put a smile on my face.

39
STILL ALIVE IN '95

Another new year began. I was still at *Penthouse* and making more money than ever! I was headed towards my thirtieth birthday in the fall and I was starting to think I would never get out of that company. Sure, I could have just quit, but I didn't have the guts. I couldn't bring myself to walk away from a great salary, especially when I was still extremely underqualified for any similar positions at a real company. They tend to want their accounting and finance people to have college degrees in, well, you know, accounting or finance. I had failed my way up the ladder here, luckily, but I was never going to make that kind of money anywhere else, so I stayed. And I drank. A lot.

Despite the influx of cash the bond sale had brought in, we still were in a deep financial hole. That led to Bob having to sell his building at 66th and Broadway where *Penthouse* had been headquartered for decades. We moved to a crappy building over on Park Avenue. Well, the building wasn't crappy, but our space within it certainly was. The wise move would have been to move someplace with much lower rent, maybe even take the whole operation to Jersey or anywhere cheaper than Manhattan. But it just wasn't in their blood. They thought the Park Avenue address would help them keep up appearances. Never mind that we had to squeeze employees into every nook and cranny of a space clearly not designed for this many people.

Tim and his phone sex division were still doing well, but they were one of the few profit centers making good money. The rest of the place was bleeding cash. Eventually, they shut down *Longevity Magazine*. Budgets were slashed in every department. Even the men in brown polyester sport coats found their department decimated. My bookie, Champ, got kicked to the curb. Luckily, my poor gambling skills still gave him plenty of pocket money.

It was a dark time for the empire. And yet I was having a blast! I knew that the end was near so I ate, drank and was merry. I picked up a few bartending shifts to make some extra coin and doubled down on my serious drinking.

I finally started matching the lifestyle of the *Mad Men* era guys I'd started working with seven years earlier. Liquid lunches were becoming more recurring. Then I'd head to the bar and keep the party going. Working a nine-to-five day job and hanging out with bartenders is not a lifestyle I recommend. I was constantly in need of sleep. Since I'd stopped caring about my job, I logged endless vacation days and sick days. I'd walk out of the office on a Wednesday, head down to the bar and end up calling in sick from Atlantic City the next morning.

The worst day came on one particular Friday. I'd been out the Thursday night before drinking with my fellow bartenders until closing time, and then went with them to an after-hours joint over on Third Avenue. This was something I often did on Fridays and Saturdays, but not on a Thursday. We were out until almost sunrise the next morning. As I stumbled home I planned on leaving a message at the office calling in sick, but in my drunken haze I remembered that I had to go in to run a report. It was the only semi-important thing I was still in charge of and I had to go in and get it done. I hurried into bed and set my alarm. Two hours later I shambled into the office, not just hung over, but still drunk. Really, really drunk. I tried to nonchalantly sneak past everyone on the way to my office, like a ramshackle Inspector Clouseau. I garnered more attention in my poor attempts to go unnoticed than I did on a normal morning. I finally made it to my office and shut the door. I thought I was going to throw up. I sat at my desk and with shaky hands ran the computer reports that needed to get done. An hour later I emerged from my office, which now smelled like the floor of a messy brewery and loudly announced to no one in particular that I had to go to a meeting across town. I went home, collapsed and didn't wake up until midnight.

I'm sure Pete and Tim weren't too thrilled with my erratic behavior, but they didn't really come down on me too hard. Pete had bigger things to worry about since he was the CFO of a company mired in millions of dollars of debt. And Tim, while I'm sure he was a little pissed that I was being a dick, could see my side of things. He, too, knew the end was near, but he had a wife and a family to think about, so he had to play the corporate angle and ride it out until the bitter end.

40
THE END

Then one day Tim invited me out to lunch. This wasn't that unusual since we would go drink beers and complain about our situation at least once a week at a watering hole just far enough away from the new office that we knew we'd never bump into anyone. But on this day, he was a little bit off. I didn't know what it was until our beers came. He raised his to salute me, and said he was sad to tell me that my name was on the list. I knew what he meant right away. We were doing another big round of layoffs and Kathy had added my name to the list. My inability to follow through on saving *Omni* had come back to bite me on the ass. After all of the near misses and close calls, this was it. I was finally going to be let go.

As much as I'd been expecting it, the news still stung. I'd been there for almost eight years. It was the only real company I'd ever worked at. And soon it would be over. He said he wasn't supposed to tell me and that I had to keep it under my hat until the axe officially came down, which would probably be within a week. I thanked him for telling me and for being a good guy for all the years he'd been my boss and the last few where he hadn't, but still lent me a helping hand. He was a good man and we drank and reminisced for the rest of the afternoon.

In true *Penthouse* style, even my firing didn't go professionally. They kept putting off the layoffs, adding more names to the list. But there was no doubt I was going. More names were being added, none were being taken off. And I was on top of the list. Number one with a bullet. I actually tried to clean up my act after that. The realization that I would soon be unemployed sobered me up quite a bit. I had the safety net of bartending shifts to fall back on, but now that it was my only option I wasn't sure that was a path I wanted to go down either.

I started trying to figure out what I was going to do with the rest of my life. I'd just turned thirty, had almost no money in the bank, a useless degree in psychology and seven-plus years of a finance career at a company in ruins. My only real drinking at that point was at frequent lunches with Tim as we commiserated about our lives. He was stuck riding the Dr. Strangelove missile into the ground because he had to support his family. I had no such worries, but I was still pretty worried about where my rent money was going to come from.

A month went by and I was still employed. Tim took me to lunch again one Monday, and when the beers came, he raised his glass in salute once more.

"It's tomorrow," he said.

And that was that. I'd already removed most of the personal effects from my office, but one day's notice gave me enough time to prep myself. We drank and cheered each other up for different reasons.

Our one memorable discussion was about another person he had to let go. This had come up a few times over the past four weeks where I acted as a sounding board for him as he helped decide who would stay and who would be let go. This last instance was in the ad services department. It came down to which of two young women would be laid off. Both made the same salary and did the same job. One was better at it than the other, but had been there less time. We both agreed that the fair thing would be to base it on seniority and keep the one who had been there the longest. It was the right thing to do. Unfortunately, the person we decided to let go was Kelly, who I had flirted with ever so briefly the prior year. I felt terrible that I was partly responsible for her losing her job, but that's just the way these things go. Tim and I continued our drunken Viking farewell and promised to stay in touch.

The next morning, I sat staring blankly out the window for an hour or so until Pete called me into his office. The poor guy was flustered. I think he'd really grown to like me over the years and felt bad that he was about to fire me. That and the fact that his own future was in dire peril had him on edge as well. I made it easier on the guy.

"I'm fired, right? I can just go chat with HR."

He shook his head yes and was quite relieved.

I went through the HR process as quickly as I could. The severance package they offered me was four months salary. Not bad, but far less than I'd seen people there for much less time get paid out. I sat wondering if I should fight for more, but convincing myself it wasn't worth the struggle. Then the HR woman said, and of course you'll get paid for any unused vacation and sick days. She pulled out my file and said, "Okay, according to your file, you haven't used any of your days and still have some carried over from the prior year." She did a quick calculation and said that meant I'd get another month's salary. Now I knew for a fact that I'd taken copious amounts of sick days and vacation days that year with reckless, drunken abandon. Probably double or even triple what I was allowed. So either Tim had gone in and adjusted my file as one final tip of his cap, or, in true *Penthouse* style, they just didn't know what the hell was going on. I signed my paperwork and walked out the door. I stopped by a couple of offices along the way to say a few quick goodbyes. Some of the other folks who were being simultaneously let go agreed to gather their belongings and meet at a nearby bar.

My last stop before leaving was the department Tim and I had discussed the day before. All the girls were there, including Kelly. They'd all heard that I'd been let go and said they would meet us at lunch for a farewell beer. Kelly still had not yet been told about her own future.

When I got to the bar, the mood was pretty somber. I was the only one there who had known for weeks that the end was coming so the other folks were in a state of shock. Before long it was lunchtime and the folks who still had jobs came in and the mood picked up. The girls from the ad department came in. Kelly spotted me and was laughing, "Hey, you won't believe it! I got fired too!!"

"Yeah, I heard," I said, as Tim walked in and bought everyone a round of drinks. The party was just starting, but my eight-year journey had finally come to a close. I didn't really know what the future held, but I have to admit I felt relieved. I knew I wasn't cut out to be an accountant and definitely not in the erotica/porn industry. Getting fired had finally pushed me out into the real world and it was time to get out of there and see what I could really do. The next stage of my life was about to begin.

EPILOGUE

As the nineties came to an end, Bob Guccione's situation continued its downward spiral, both personally and professionally. His longtime partner, and my personal nemesis, Kathy Keeton, passed away in 1997. General Media Inc. struggled on for a few more years, but was unable to dig out from under the mountain of debt and interest payments related to the bond offerings that were supposed to save the company. *Penthouse Magazine* was sold in a bankruptcy sale in 2003 and continues to be published as a pale imitation of its powerhouse past. Bob Guccione lost his stately Manhattan house and his company, a company that had earned an estimated four billion dollars in his lifetime. He eventually succumbed to the throat and lung cancer that for the last few years of his life robbed him of that deep, beautiful voice that had served him so well over the years. Rest in peace, Bob. I would not be who I am today had our paths not crossed.

My final day at *Penthouse* was November 7, 1995. I'm happy to report that my life actually turned out pretty great. I moved on to another eight-year misadventure on the finance side of the publishing world, when I lucked into a job at Time Inc. (at half the salary I was making at *Penthouse*, but I was happy to get it). Once again I worked my way up through the company and reached the role of corporate vice president.

Another long stint of being a numbers guy proved one thing: I was *definitely* not cut out to be a numbers guy. Instead of burying my head in the sand like I did at the end of my *Penthouse* stint, I actually did something about it. I succumbed to my inner demons and my creative muse and sought out a life as a writer and performer. After having enough success to think I was on the right path, I finally shook off the corporate shackles forever in 2004 and never looked back.

I am now a working writer and semi-successful actor. Last year I made less than what I made that first year at *Penthouse*, but I'm the happiest I've ever been. My time with the Gooch and company will always be a cherished part of my life.

Most importantly, on that final night of drinking and goodbyes after we both lost our jobs, Kelly and I ended up sitting next to each other and the flirtation started up anew. We went out on our first date a week later and have been together ever since. We've been married almost fifteen years now and have a beautiful family and a wonderful life together.

All the result of my unexpectedly blessed *Penthouse* past.

After a sixteen-year, soul-crushing career as a corporate executive, Steve Belanger found salvation in a life of writing and performing. He is currently a contributing editor at *Men's Health Magazine* and is the host of *The Men's Health Podcast*. After his eight-year experience at *Penthouse*, Steve went on to a successful career at Time Inc. where he oversaw such iconic titles as *Field & Stream* and *Popular Science*. He was a corporate vice president there in 2004 when he decided to walk away from it all in search of more creative pursuits. He has worked with Oscar-winners, appeared on numerous TV shows and written countless scripts. His work has appeared in several major magazines and he has performed comedy on the country's most celebrated stages. Steve is based in Long Island, NY, but spends a lot of time on both coasts kissing asses and furthering his career.

Follow Steve on Twitter: @stevebelanger

Made in United States
North Haven, CT
19 April 2022

18396354R00117